T0009272

Transform to a hopeful, energized "normal" by hardwiring your brain to work positively *for* you, rather than against you. Weissenbacher's innovative steps—backed by neuroscience and real-life application—bypass emotional roadblocks, triggers for destructive thoughts and actions, and pave the path toward freedom, joy, and lasting change.

Dr. Kevin Leman, internationally known veteran psychologist and *New York Times* bestselling author of more than fifty books, including *The Birth Order Book, Have a New Kid by Friday*, and *Sheet Music*

Insightful and blessedly practical, this hope-filled book offers vital keys to the ultimate prize: changing ourselves with God's help.

Jeff Lucas, author, speaker, broadcaster

Dr. Weissenbacher integrates discoveries in the field of neuroscience with the unchanging truth of Scripture to address the struggles of anyone seeking to make personal changes. By educating the reader as to why change is difficult, he helps to relieve the burdens of shame and failure that often occur. He includes an action plan that applies to any harmful, negative, or destructive behavior, including negative thinking, substance abuse, pornography addiction, disordered eating, overspending, media addiction, or any other behavior interfering with one's relationship with God and others.

Joyce Williams, MS, LPC, founder of Light of the Rockies Christian Counseling Center

In *The Brain Change Program*, Dr. Alan Weissenbacher writes from his professional experience with addiction recovery programs and offers new and better tools to find physical, psychological, and spiritual healing. In this gentle, empowering, compelling, and humorous yet poignant account, Weissenbacher brings together his doctoral research in spiritual healing and neuroscience with years of practical experience as a counselor. The result is authentic, realistic help to overcome destructive thoughts, be free from addiction, and improve your spiritual life.

Dr. Robert Russell, founding director of the Center for Theology and the Natural Sciences

Alan Weissenbacher is the rare combination of scientist, theologian, and field minister. He combines his grasp of the sciences, his profound respect for people with different perspectives, and his personal concern for others. While accessible to any reader, *The Brain Change Program* also commands the respect of the specialist. His book guides readers to a faith-based understanding of brain science, separating it from "pop psychology," and equips them with the ability to effect change in their lives.

Dr. Earl Creps, director of the Center for Leadership Studies at Northwest University

At a time when people's mental, emotional, and spiritual health has worn thin, Alan offers a realistic and hopeful means to finding wholeness. This practical guide is built on Alan's many years of experience working with deeply fractured people, and it is a confluence of carefully studied neuroscience, Christian theology, and spiritual formation. It is rare for an author to successfully bring together various expertise, which is why I have utilized Alan's help in teaching and training people in my own church.

Brent Cunningham, pastor of spiritual formation, Timberline Church, Colorado

Change does not just happen, and the science behind change can be difficult to explain. In *The Brain Change Program*, Dr. Alan Weissenbacher has merged neuroscience with steps for meaningful change into one accessible resource. Using scientific research, Dr. Weissenbacher honors the difficulties inherent to change and provides practical steps and tools that lead to true change. This valuable resource explains why common yet ineffective methods do not effect change but instead enforce resistance to change. *The Brain Change Program* grounded and enriched my use of imagination and prayer toward transformational change. This book is a gift to anyone in the business of helping people become their best selves. It changed me, and it will do the same for you and those you serve.

Ellen Martin, personal and professional coach, author of *A Life Shared: Meaningful Conversations with Our Kids*

In this terrific work, Alan Weissenbacher has skillfully integrated his clinical experiences with his extensive studies in neuroscience and theology in a delightful and encouraging manner. The valuable insights contained in this book will certainly be of great help to people struggling with personal change.

Junghyung Kim, *associate professor of philosophy of religion, Yonsei University, Korea*

In *The Brain Change Program*, Dr. Alan Weissenbacher draws to our attention something we use every day but don't necessarily think about: the brain. This practical resource helps us approach how we think and behave, making us more conscientious of our minds and habits and more positive, productive people. You will learn to think about the brain differently and, as a result, learn to live differently—and for the better.

T. Shane Couch, MAR, CPSAS, Missionaries to Ministers, Inc.

Since COVID, the rates of depression and mental distress have skyrocketed. Thankfully, Alan is an expert in the field of rewiring the brain in order to overcome self-destructive thoughts, habits, and addictions. He has always been a student of behavior, thought, and the connection between the two. His brilliance is easily camouflaged, as he is a master of taking a complex subject and making it simple for others to understand. Alan's book will revolutionize the way that society moves forward from the pandemic, both inside and outside of the church.

Jeff Sandstrom, executive pastor, Victory City Church, Chicago, Illinois

The Brain Change Program

6 Steps to Renew Your Mind and Transform Your Life

DR. ALAN WEISSENBACHER

BroadStreet
P U B L I S H I N G

BroadStreet Publishing® Group, LLC
Savage, Minnesota, USA
BroadStreetPublishing.com

The Brain Change Program:
6 Steps to Renew Your Mind and Transform Your Life

Copyright © 2024 Dr. Alan Weissenbacher

9781424566624 (hardcover)
9781424566631 (ebook)

All rights reserved. No part of this book may be reproduced in any form, except for brief quotations in printed reviews, without permission in writing from the publisher.

Names and certain identifying details have been changed to protect the confidentiality of individuals, except where a person has given direct permission to use their real name.

Scripture quotations marked NIV are taken from The Holy Bible, New International Version® NIV®. Copyright © 1973, 1978, 1984, 2011 by Biblica, Inc.™ Used by permission. All rights reserved worldwide. Scripture quotations marked ESV are taken from the ESV® Bible (The Holy Bible, English Standard Version®), copyright © 2001 by Crossway, a publishing ministry of Good News Publishers. Used by permission. All rights reserved. Scripture quotations marked NASB are taken from the New American Standard Bible® (NASB), Copyright © 1960, 1962, 1963, 1968, 1971, 1972, 1973, 1975, 1977, 1995, 2020 by The Lockman Foundation. Used by permission. www.Lockman.org. Scripture quotations marked NLT are taken from the Holy Bible, New Living Translation (NLT). Copyright © 1996, 2004, 2015 by Tyndale House Foundation. Used by permission of Tyndale House Publishers, a Division of Tyndale House Ministries, Carol Stream, Illinois, 60188. All rights reserved.

Cover and interior by Garborg Design Works | garborgdesign.com

Printed in China

24 25 26 27 28 5 4 3 2 1

I dedicate this book to the courageous clients of the Denver Rescue Mission and the Harvest Farm rehabilitation program. Your bravery in asking for help, your desire for change, your perseverance through setbacks, and your joy in victories inspired this work. So, dear reader, if anything in this book helps you achieve positive change in your life and you wish to give back, I encourage you to support programs like the Denver Rescue Mission in your local area.

Contents

Preface 10

Introduction 15

Chapter 1: Life Change 20

This Is Not a Solo Project 23

Chapter 2: Use It or Lose It 26

Neural Plasticity 29

Brain Training 30

Constructing and Deconstructing Pathways 33

The Failure of Willpower 36

Automaticity 38

Shaping Personal Character 39

Training to Forgive 41

Failure and Perseverance 45

Developing Spiritual Discipline 48

Praying Forward 50

Dark Night of the Soul 52

Summary 53

Chapter 3: Neurons that Fire Together, Wire Together 57

Neural Linking 58

Triggers 62

Rewiring Neural Links 64

Creating a New Worldview 66

Training Behaviors, Emotions, and Morals 70

Emotional Reframing 75

Reframing and Forgiveness 77

Culture Shock 79

Achieving Positive Impact 85

The Power of Personal Testimonies 88

Counseling 90

Summary 92

Chapter 4: The Power of the Imagination 96

Practice Makes Automatic, Not Perfect 101

The Power of Perception 102

Imagination and Moral Development 105

Summary 117

Chapter 5: The 6-Step Brain Change Program 121

Step 1: Identify the Thought 124

Step 2: Evaluate 126

Step 3: Replace, Don't Resist 127

Step 4: Retrain with Imagination 128

Step 5: Introduce a New Element 128

Step 6: Repeat, Rehearse, Repeat 130

The Brain Change Program in Action 131

The Fight Phase 158

Escaping the Flames 162

Summary 163

Acknowledgments 165

Endnotes 166

About the Author 175

Preface

"Hey, y'all. I just want you to know that only chumps work when there's Social Security. It's been fun. Thanks for the three hot meals and a cot. Crack, whiskey, and the streets of Vegas are calling me. I'm outta here."

Those were Raymond's final words during his graduation speech before leaving the Denver Rescue Mission's Harvest Farm addiction rehabilitation program. Stunned, his audience sat in silence. Raymond strutted out, climbed into the car gifted to him by his church, and drove away.

Before coming to our program, Raymond had been living on the streets and battling alcohol and cocaine addictions for years. At our program, though, he was a model client who demonstrated the efficacy of spiritual-based rehabilitation. Raymond took to the program's Christian content, devouring Scripture, mentoring other residents, and leading various social work projects to help clients give back to the community. He worked hard in our farm setting and underwent intensive individual counseling, job training, and group therapy. My heart swelled at my favorite memory of Raymond—when he led other clients in building an orphanage in Juarez, Mexico. Everyone saved what little money they had to purchase toys for the orphanage so that it had more to offer the kids than just walls.

Raymond's bombshell of a decision and departing words devastated the current residents, many of whom were just beginning the program and looking for inspiration. I watched as hope dimmed in their eyes. Their thoughts were written across their glum faces: *If the superstar failed, what chance do we have? Will we spend two useless years here too?* Members of his church had also come to support him on his big day, and they, too, were brokenhearted. How could this have happened?

Of course, the situation dismayed the counselors and staff as well—not only because they suddenly needed to revive a sense of hope in a room of more than fifty clients before they also chose to throw in the towel, but also because we questioned ourselves. How did we miss this? Could we have said something different? Did we pray enough for Raymond? The members of his church invested considerable time, effort, and community into this man only to watch all of it crumble before their eyes. Not to mention they probably wanted to chase the guy down and retrieve the car. Would they be willing to mentor and invest in someone else after this?

I compare Raymond's experience to another resident, Charles. Charles had been my client for six months and frustrated me at every turn. He spent hours arguing with me over simple rules, such as showing up to work on time and performing basic hygiene. He initially despised the program's Christian content and fought hard against the spiritual requirements. He maintained the minimum expectations to retain his residency—but just barely.

Eventually, Charles reached success in the program. I remember the day he ran into my office after returning from his monthly evaluation at the state mental hospital. "Guess what, guess what!" he shouted before brandishing an official-looking piece of paper. "I am now certified mental-illness free! The state mental health board has affirmed that all five mental illnesses are gone!" Grinning, he said, "I have an official government document declaring me legally sane. Do you?"

How did Raymond, a model client, achieve such a miraculous life change only to crash and burn? And yet Charles, a challenging client formerly known by people in town as the man who wore green cowboy boots while yelling at the air, overcame a methamphetamine addiction and permanently changed his life for the better. What marks the difference between those who claim victory and those who succumb to failure, and not just addicts, but anyone desiring to make a change in their life?

I worked in the field of addiction therapy for years. I regularly met with people whose brains suffered damage from substance abuse but who wanted to free themselves from their addictions. They came to us broken, many having spent years living on the streets, and their destructive behaviors had cost them everything: money, homes, jobs, family, and friends. Not to mention their greatest need: healing from the pains that contributed to their addictions in the first place.

It is easy to blame people who fail. Their hearts are hardened. They are stony ground (see Mark 4:5). But are they really? Some people conclude that those who fail simply didn't work hard enough, but how many of us fail at important things despite all our hard work? What if we need a different approach? One that can soften "stony ground" and increase the likelihood that hard work will pay off. What if the problem is less about hardened hearts, stony ground, and hard work and more about the need for us to provide people with better tools for change?

I'm inspired by the matter of who succeeds and who fails, those whose transformations of character are aided by Christian content and those for whom Christian content shows no effect. And while my initial questions were designed to improve Christian addiction recovery programs, ultimately, my main question was how we can help people grow in their ability to be like Christ, control their brain, overcome sin, develop successful spiritual practices, and find joy in outward-directed service to others. Unfortunately, I couldn't find the answers in my rehabilitation role alone, so I eventually resigned from my position at the rehabilitation center to study the brain.

My search for answers led to a host of discoveries that offered insight on various spiritual questions: After I have made the decision to forgive someone, why do I still feel so angry? How does memorizing Scripture help me overcome a bad habit? Why do I keep doing that which I do not want to do? Why does willpower fail? Am I sinning in my thoughts when temptation comes to mind? How can I pray better? How can I stop wandering thoughts? I know God loves me, but why don't I feel it? And how can I renew my mind and take thoughts captive?

Recent discoveries in neuroscience helped me answer these questions, and I unpack them in the chapters to follow. The good news is that we *can* change our brain and free ourselves from destructive thoughts and harmful behaviors and toward that which produces the fruit of the Spirit: love, joy, peace, patience, kindness, goodness, faithfulness, gentleness, and self-control. With God, we truly have the power to renew our minds and transform our lives.

> With God, we truly have the power to renew our minds and transform our lives.

Introduction

So many people want to make changes in their lives but don't know how. We're often told that we just need the willpower to change, to pull ourselves up by our bootstraps. And when that fails, we blame ourselves.

In Christian circles, we are also told that in order to change we must renew our minds (Romans 12:2) and take every thought captive (2 Corinthians 10:5). These statements typically left me personally discouraged because how exactly do I accomplish these things? I wanted a blueprint! Anyone who's ever tried to fall asleep while their brain incessantly reminds them of their problems and shortcomings knows that taking thoughts captive is much easier said than done. But! It can be done.

Where Are the Technical Details?

Typically, books about the brain, behaviors, and beliefs dedicate pages upon pages to thoroughly exploring specific areas of the brain and explaining in great detail what they do, such as the amygdala's involvement in the fear response or the various brain regions correlated with mystical religious experiences. There are certainly areas of specificity in the brain and a degree of shared commonality among persons when it comes to behavior and experiences, but I chose to mostly forgo the specifics.

Instead, I look at the brain as a whole—its plasticity and ability to learn, the subsequent altering of its shape, and the strengthening of connectivity to accommodate learning and change. Plasticity refers to the brain's ability to physically transform itself through the activities it performs, making future actions and thoughts easier or harder depending on the nature of the transformation. Don't worry; we'll thoroughly explore all of these concepts and more in the chapters to come.

We cannot and should not assume, however, that the brain and its functions are wholly understood by the scientific community. Researchers continue to make discoveries regarding the mechanism of neural plasticity as well as the generation of new neurons. Still, these new and emerging discoveries do not invalidate or make null and void my approach to change because mine does not rely on the idea that plasticity operates in a specific or singular manner. My strategies merely recognize that plasticity exists and plays a powerful role in learning, growing, and experiencing life.

I believe our knowledge of the brain should go beyond understanding mental processes to also understanding how these processes integrate to produce and maintain who a person is and who they can become. I, of course, provide references to scientific literature where appropriate for those who wish to explore all the technical details.

Our knowledge of the brain should go beyond understanding mental processes to also understanding how these processes integrate to produce and maintain who a person is and who they can become.

The Road Map

The journey of learning to take your thoughts captive and renew your mind begins in Chapter 2, which contains a basic summary of how the brain forms and transforms itself through the activities it performs. By understanding how the brain changes, you can harness the ability to form it in the direction you wish, away from certain thoughts, emotions, and behaviors and toward others. In this same chapter, I explain why we persist in doing things we don't want to do and how to stop this habit.

Subsections in Chapter 2 explain why willpower fails; how you can change your approach to willpower to maximize your chances for success; how understanding the way the brain learns and develops can help you grow in prayer, forgiveness, and other spiritual disciplines; how to practice these spiritual disciplines more effectively, and how to cope when you're struggling to connect with God.

In Chapter 3 we explore how the brain forges connections so that we can better understand how our emotions impact our behavior. We learn how to move past emotional roadblocks and triggers that provoke destructive thoughts and actions.

We also discover in Chapter 3 how our past experiences condition what we see and remember. We tend to only see what our life has trained us to see, and if we have only done negative training—training that teaches us to only see a punishing God, for example, or that no one likes us or that the world works against us or that all homeless people are lazy—then how can we expect to see anything different? We only notice data that support our existing beliefs. How do we change our inability to see that which can change our outlook?

I discuss implications for altering behavior, counseling, forgiveness, community service, and overcoming culture shock. Culture shock doesn't just occur when moving to new cultures. Anyone molding their life into something new will inevitably experience some form of culture shock. For example, sometimes the inability to recover from addiction stems from the culture shock of sober living.

In Chapter 4 I talk about the power of imagination and its key role in life transformation, moral education, and improving spiritual disciplines. Your brain cannot tell the difference between imagining an action and actually doing it, so you can change your brain in your imagination as easily as you could through actual performance.

Chapter 5 then pulls together all of the primary takeaways from each previous chapter and weaves them into a comprehensive six-step brain change program. This program will not only help you identify the change you wish to make, but it will also empower you to put steps into practice to make the change happen—and endure.

I pray that everyone who reads this book gains insight into how to improve their spiritual lives by understanding the brain. This is not a magical procedure for health, wealth, and enlightenment. It is rather a discipline of controlling and guiding the brain to produce Christlike character, help others, and find joy therein.

Chapter 1

Life Change: Microwave or Crock-Pot?

Change typically occurs gradually with both progress and setbacks, yet at the same time, short-term, dramatic change does occasionally happen. In the Bible, we read of two types of change programs that I like to call the Paul Program and the Jacob Program.

> Change typically occurs gradually with both progress and setbacks.

The Paul Program, found in Acts 9 of the Bible, illustrates dramatic change in a short period of time. Saul, later more widely known as Paul, was engaged in a holy war against the

Christian church, running rampant and killing believers. One day, while on his way to arrest followers of Jesus, a light from heaven knocked him to the ground. He had a conversation with Jesus that changed him as a person, so much so that those who knew him couldn't believe it. He went from killing Christians to writing much of the New Testament and preaching about Jesus across Europe and Asia.

At the Denver Rescue Mission, the addiction rehabilitation center at which I worked for years, many people would pray for instantaneous change like Paul's, hoping God would zap away their drug craving in an instant, freeing them from the struggle. While this type of change does happen, it's rare. It occurs often enough, though, for everyone to want to join the Paul Program. Who can blame them? Many of us are no different: *God, take away my anger, lust, or help me make peace with my grief by tomorrow*. I want that type of change, too, when it comes to improving areas of my life. Microwave me into righteousness, God!

Most of us, however, are on the second type of change program: the Jacob Program. That is, we do not experience the microwave change but rather the slow and steady incremental change that takes place inside a Crock-Pot. The Jacob Program, illustrated in Genesis 25–32, involves slow change—with struggle.

Jacob lied and cheated to steal his brother Esau's birthright and blessing before fleeing from Esau and his anger. Jacob eventually worked for his uncle, Laban, who proved just as deceitful as Jacob. Laban's deception first comes through in his treatment of

Jacob after Jacob fell in love with Laban's daughter, Rachel. Jacob agreed to work for seven years in exchange for Rachel's hand in marriage, but Laban instead tricked him into marrying his other daughter, Leah. Laban then forced Jacob to work another seven years for Rachel. Although men commonly had multiple wives back then, this marital arrangement caused problems for Jacob.

Add to these deceptions a few more years of work during which Laban repeatedly changed the terms of their agreement regarding Jacob's wages (Genesis 31:7), and Jacob ended up working twenty years because of Laban's deceit. In short, Jacob the Deceiver became Jacob the Deceived. At the end of this period, Jacob fought with God, and afterward God changed Jacob's name to Israel, revealing Jacob's new identity. His final wrestling match with God may very well symbolize the twenty years he spent wrestling with his uncle, himself, and God, all of which changed Jacob's character. If you are interested in the details of the story, I direct you to Genesis chapters 29–30.

I often narrated these two Bible stories to my clients. "If God has not zapped you so that your addiction is gone, then you are probably on the Jacob Program," I'd say. "This means you are in boot camp for change."

The Jacob Program is not a bad thing or something to feel disappointed about. A person who miraculously changes overnight does have a great testimony that glorifies God, but who would you rather have as a mentor: someone who changed overnight or someone who fought a long, grueling battle and emerged victorious? A person who has wrestled and won has not only experienced much but also has wisdom to impart.

So, yes, pray for rapid change but be ready to wrestle. And if you are wrestling, take courage, for you have much to learn in the journey and much to offer others.

Pray for rapid change but be ready to wrestle.

This Is Not a Solo Project

Knowing that we can, in fact, change our brains may lead some people to believe that they can solve all their issues within the privacy of their own bedroom: *Yes! I don't have to let others know that I am anything but perfect. I can maintain the façade of having it all together while quietly working on my prevailing issues in secret.* I admit this sounds appealing.

Many of us, myself included, do not want to appear weak. But the more people you have on your brain-change team, the more likely you are to succeed and make those positive changes permanent. Not only can others encourage you, but they can also shed light on areas in need of change that you might not yet be aware of. After all, we can be masters at deceiving ourselves.

The more people you have on your brain-change team, the more likely you are to succeed and make those positive changes permanent.

It's also important to note that some brain pathways go so deep and are so strong that you, alone, cannot change them. My clients in addiction therapy are prime examples. It is highly unlikely that addicts can independently change years or decades of addictive behaviors. Success is more likely when they attend small support groups, seek professional help, or check in to a full-on treatment center if necessary.

But if you are not an addict or if there are no professional programs that offer help and support for whatever plagues you, then find a church group and let it serve as your "treatment center." Share your struggles with others whom you trust so that they, too, can help you. You don't need to, nor should you, do this alone. You may be so stuck in brain ruts that change is impossible without the support of others.

Think of home or car repairs. Maybe you can re-caulk a bathtub, but you need a professional technician when it comes to replacing an HVAC system. You may know how to change the oil in your car, but an auto repair shop will change it much faster, and you probably need a mechanic for serious repairs. To further extend this example, the need for some necessary repairs can go unnoticed, and without periodic checkups on your vehicle, you risk jeopardizing its ability to drive. It is better to have help in identifying and resolving issues proactively—before the wheels fall off!

I used to pray, *God speak to me.* Then I asked myself why I was trying to limit God to one-on-one interactions strictly within the context of prayer. The more avenues available to God to reach me, the better. So I changed my prayer: *God, do not speak directly to me only in some still, small voice, but speak through my wife, my children, my boss, that strange guy I see every day on the train, the neighbor's beagle…whatever it takes!*

God's primary approach to working in your life may involve other people, and God may use you as the primary approach, the vehicle, to reach someone else. We need others to help us identify the parts of ourselves in need of change and to help motivate us to make our brain changes stick.

> God's primary approach to working in your life may involve other people, and God may use you as the primary approach, the vehicle, to reach someone else.

As you begin your brain change journey, I strongly encourage you to establish a support system. The positive feelings that come from supportive friends go a long way.

Reflect

1. Read and think through the last half of 2 Corinthians 10:5: "taking every thought captive to the obedience of Christ" (NASB). What thoughts do you want to take captive?

2. How effective have you been at stopping negative thoughts? What strategies do you use?

3. In what area(s) of your life have you felt as though you've been in a long-term wrestling match or struggle? How does the story of Jacob bring you hope?

Chapter 2

Use It or Lose It: Neurons, Pathways, and Habits, Oh My

I was meeting with Harold at his apartment, searching for a place to sit among his many leather working tools. Sadly, our conversation was not about this new hobby he'd picked up while in recovery but about his recent relapse. He refused to meet my gaze and instead stared down at a half-finished belt, twisting it in his hands.

"Were you depressed?" I asked.

"No," he replied, twisting the belt harder.

"Lonely?"

"No."

"Were you angry about something?"

"No."

After going through a litany of possible scenarios that might have emotionally contributed to his relapse, he finally blurted out, "There was no reason! I was feeling fine. I was just walking down the sidewalk past the bar I used to go to. Next thing I knew, I was in my usual seat, drinking my usual poison, and my year and a half of sobriety was gone. I don't remember opening the door or anything."

How did Harold turn into a robot that did exactly what he *didn't* want to do? To figure this out, we have to look at the brain. The brain has over one hundred billion nerve cells and over one trillion support cells with over a quadrillion connections among them. Until recently, most scientists thought the brain, with all its cells and connections, was a hardwired machine incapable of change. The prevailing thought was that the brain stopped growing around age eighteen and only slowly declined with age. And any lost cells or connections never returned. But beginning in the 1960s and '70s, various scientific discoveries revealed that the brain physically transforms itself with the activities it performs, rewiring and perfecting its circuitry. I'll share plenty of examples of this throughout this chapter, so stick with me.

The brain creates new neurons, lays down new circuits, and forms new connections and branches that carry messages to and from other neurons. At the same time, it removes unused connections and prunes dormant or unused neurons, much like the owner of a houseplant will prune dead and dying leaves.

To illustrate this pruning process, imagine a new neuron develops and then heads out into the great wide world of your brain in search of a home where it can attach and grow. Let's say the new neuron heads over to the area in your brain responsible for kindness. Because you're already a kind person, the new neuron arrives and sees plenty of kindness neurons hustling and bustling with activity. The new neuron says, "Wow! So much activity! These neurons must need help." Your new neuron will then connect, grow, and become part of the hard-working crew in this area of the brain. And by gaining a new neuron in this area, your kindness grows and strengthens, and kind responses become even more instinctual.

If, however, the brain belongs to a consistently mean person, the new neuron arriving in the kindness area will find low activity and say, "Oh, the productivity in the kindness area is so slow that this neglected area might be ready to close up shop. No reason to attach here." The neuron then fails to connect, dissolves, and is reabsorbed by the body.

New neurons are attracted to active, frequently used areas of your brain but do little with inactive, seldomly used areas. But you have the power to alter activity levels in areas of your brain. If the mean person, for example, consciously puts forth the effort to practice kindness, then the kindness area will attract new neurons, and the boost in activity will convince new neurons to attach and become part of the kindness work crew.

Neural Plasticity

Alterations in the brain come from more than adding and removing neurons. Existing neurons can also change. This is, in part, how we transform our brain and the actions associated with it: by exercising choice in our thoughts and behaviors. Neurons become stronger through repeated use and weakened through inattention, so we know that they are malleable. Said in another way, continually stimulating a neuron increases its ability to respond, and repeatedly neglecting a neuron weakens its ability to respond. This ability is called neural plasticity.

Let's say you want to learn French, so you start learning and practicing the language. As a result, a bunch of your neurons start to develop in relation to French. They start out weak, and you face challenges as you learn, but as French neurons become stronger and faster, you find it easier to use the language. Eventually you're able to speak French fluently or maybe even dream in French. However, if years go by without practice, you will have probably forgotten a lot of the language when you try to use it again. By neglecting these French neurons, they weaken.

Like muscles, frequently used neurons get stronger, and unused neurons atrophy. They follow the "use it or lose it" concept. A helpful, often-used metaphor that explains how the brain works is sledding down a snowy hill. The hill itself and whatever obstacles may be on it, like trees or bumps, symbolize our genetics, or our starting point. Then, when we sled down the hill, we inevitably leave paths in the snow wherever we choose to steer.

If we spend an entire afternoon sledding, then we'll have worn deep grooves into the snowy paths we steered down most.

> Like muscles, frequently used neurons get stronger, and unused neurons atrophy. They follow the "use it or lose it" concept.

We lay down mental paths in a similar way. When we choose the same thought or make the same choice over and over again, we create a rut in our mental path that can be tricky to get out of. Then, try as we might to steer another course, we slide into the rut and follow it all the way down the hill.

We can forge new paths, but it's a challenging undertaking because the old paths are deeper and faster. These paths establish our habits. Repeat a thought or action long enough, and the path becomes an even deeper rut or more "neurologically entrenched." In this way, mental training is just like sledding down a snowy hill.

Brain Training

Philosopher Alicia Juarrero relates that the effect of neurons strengthening or weakening is a change in probabilities. Learning and training alters your brain structure, increasing or decreasing the likelihood that a group of neurons will fire the same way in similar situations.[1] For example, most people run from danger, but rescue personnel intuitively run toward it. They changed their automatic response through training and practice.

In neurological literature, musicians, taxi drivers, and jugglers are other prime examples of training and experience shaping the brain. All of these people show substantial changes to their brain shape and function, and these changes are a product of acquiring on-the-job skills.

Neuroscientist Eleanor Maguire found that certain regions of a taxi driver's brain were larger depending on how long the person had been driving a taxi.[2] That is, a driver with a little experience showed some neural development, but a driver with years of experience showed significantly more development—a big, new brain region. Note that these brain changes do not exist in people who do not drive cabs; they are specific to cab drivers. To put it another way, taxi drivers' brains are uniquely shaped by the actions they repeatedly perform for their job—memorizing streets, directions, and traffic patterns.

The old static model of the brain might suggest that some people are born with brains uniquely suited to driving taxis, but the reality is that you become what you do. And this doesn't strictly apply to taxi drivers but also to most other occupations. People's brains are uniquely shaped by their jobs. You could even say, "Change jobs, change your brain."

> You become what you do.

Turning to musicians, not only are their brains different from non-musicians, but instrument-specific differences also exist among them, highlighting the importance of training.[3]

Those trained in reading music had structural and functional changes in brain areas responsible for processing sequences, and this training even translated into improved functioning in sequencing tasks outside of the musical domain.[4]

Musicians also show substantially increased brain activity in regions associated with body movement when listening to musical pieces they know compared to pieces they don't know,[5] and they demonstrate higher brain activity when listening to music they've previously practiced.[6] This means that practice in a particular area results in a greater ability to recognize and respond to material within that same area in the future.

Another experiment involving musicians revealed that the earlier in life a person begins musical training, the greater their performance potential—greater than those who start later but have the same length of training.[7]

Finally, turning to jugglers, those who practiced juggling for three months showed structural changes in the brain. But when jugglers refrained from practice for three months, those changes began to disappear.[8] This shows that failure to practice results in skill regression—just like our earlier example of losing the ability to speak French by not practicing it.

Taxi drivers, musicians, and jugglers teach us about the relationship between behavior and the brain. If you memorize streets and directions, play an instrument, or develop the hand-eye coordination to toss objects into the air and catch them, then the areas in your brain that are devoted to those activities grow and strengthen.

The fact that we strengthen neurons through use shows us that the longer a behavior continues, the harder it becomes to change. Traits and behaviors are fairly easy to establish when our snowy hill only has a few shallow paths. Over time, however, we develop an increasingly furrowed hill and become more set in our ways and more resistant to change.

Constructing and Deconstructing Pathways

I now switch metaphors from a snowy hill to the construction of a cement superhighway. When I talk to people with addictions, I tell them to think of their addiction as a superhighway inside their brain and their sobriety as a narrow, dirt path laid by deer, somewhere off to the side of the highway. This dirt path is particularly small if the recovering addict is new to sobriety.

When an addict experiences stress, their brain does not choose the narrow deer path. Their brain seeks the most efficient route, the superhighway, and the addict likely defaults to their addictive thinking and behavior. It's an unfortunate biological reality that they are forced to contend with.

Pornography provides another example of a tempting neural superhighway. By consuming it repeatedly, viewers lay down a superhighway in their brain. Then, when they see a member of the opposite sex, their brains take the speedy, efficient superhighway, which leads to a lustful thought instead of a virtuous one that's been relegated to the deer path.

To change a destructive pattern of thought or behavior, you must deconstruct the harmful superhighway and expand the virtuous deer path. And it makes a difference every time you choose the path, even if you fail to stick to it. Think virtuous thoughts for thirty seconds, and you have just spent thirty seconds expanding the path. In resisting bad habits, we facilitate the creation of good ones.

> In resisting bad habits,
> we facilitate the creation of good ones.

Your brain will want to reroute to the highway, and when this happens, you must make a conscious decision to return to the path. At first, you might have to make that conscious decision ten times a minute or more, but each time you return to the small path, you remove a slab of cement from the superhighway and place it on the deer path. Eventually, you only need to switch back to the path maybe five times a minute, then a few times every ten minutes, then a few times every few days, and so on.

The ultimate goal is to convert the superhighway into a path and the path into a superhighway. This is a simplified description and far easier said than done, but you get the idea. A quote that sums up this concept nicely comes from a Twitter user who responded to a query for the best advice people received in therapy: "Old pathways are worn and easy to tread. You have to choose a new path again and again before it becomes the easier one to walk."[9]

My client, Ernest, is a perfect illustration of someone who successfully converted a small path into a superhighway. He was a master of cutting, sarcastic remarks, and his sharp tongue often landed him in trouble. While sometimes funny, Ernest's insulting wit pushed everyone away when it inevitably turned on them. He wanted to change and become a person who spoke kindly, but the negative comments would shoot out of his mouth before he could stop them. It was time for him to get serious about changing his brain, so we slammed down a roadblock on his sarcastic superhighway.

The rule that Ernest and I implemented was that he had to count to ten before he spoke—every time and with every reply—even when someone said something to him as simple as "Good morning!" At first, his change in speech surprised the people who knew him. Naturally, they found it odd having to wait for him to respond. But once Ernest explained his goal to change his long-established speech patterns, they understood and were enthusiastically supportive.

We lifted the rule after a few weeks, and just like someone who fasts from sugar and later finds it less appealing, Ernest no longer defaulted to cutting remarks. The highway, unable to function as it once did, was successfully demolished. Ernest had learned to control his speech.

It takes time to build a bad habit, an addiction, or an entrenched negative thought pattern into a superhighway, so it should come as no surprise that it also takes time to dismantle it and lay a new one. Addiction rehabilitation is a perfect example. It's often a revolving door, and it's normal for a person to go to rehab several times before their sobriety sticks. But each attempt fortifies their sober brain path a little bit more. For that reason, we can reframe feelings of failure as feelings of hope—of progress. Faithfulness in the little things creates positive brain pathways that enable us to be faithful in the bigger things (see Luke 16:10).

The Failure of Willpower

Don't think of a pink elephant. What did you just think of? Probably a pink elephant. This paradox illustrates a trap-like feature that lives inside our brain: the more we try to suppress a thought, the more intrusive it becomes. Or to return to our snowy hill metaphor, our mere thoughts have the power to lay down pathways in our brain. This, too, presents another challenge to overcoming a bad habit or sin.

When you try to resist a temptation, you end up focusing on the temptation. In doing so, you start down the mental pathway of that very sin, possibly deepening it. If you tell yourself, "I must not eat candy. I must not eat candy," then you are still thinking about candy. The craving for candy then laughs at you, strengthening its area in the brain, and now you want candy more than ever before. The harder you try to escape a brain trap like this, the further it ensnares you. In biblical terms, it becomes a "stronghold."

The key to escaping a stronghold is not to attempt to rid yourself of the struggle through sheer willpower but rather to counter it by trying something new, preferably something healthy, productive, and enjoyable. I call this "addiction replacement therapy." This approach not only grows a new brain circuit, but it also triggers a release of dopamine, a chemical in our brain that makes us feel happy, thereby rewarding the new activity and consolidating new, neural connections. In short, instead of resisting a bad habit, redirect and replace it with a new one.

The chemical reaction that unfolds from focusing on a new activity offers biological support for memorizing Scripture to help overcome strongholds. Your memorization creates a new mental furrow, and then when you're faced with temptation, the Scripture you've memorized fires louder and clearer in your mind than thoughts of temptation.

Take me, for example. I am prone to pessimism. Historically, when faced with a crisis, my default reaction was anything but one of faith. However, by meditating on Bible verses about hoping and trusting in the Lord, I now repeat those verses in my head whenever pessimistic thoughts arise. And these encouraging verses of hope drown out the negative thoughts.

I have also experienced career setbacks in my life that left me confused and discouraged, so I latched on to Psalm 37:23–24. These verses state that God directs a person's steps if they are following him, and if that person stumbles, he or she will not be destroyed. God will hold them up. Again, by repeating these verses to myself often, I drown out the discouragement. I may not understand what's going on or what's going to happen with these setbacks, but I can persevere and find peace in the knowledge that God will guide me. Even if I screw up, I know that all is not lost.

Automaticity

Let's return to the story from the beginning of this chapter about Harold, who visited his usual bar and relapsed. Clearly, he had deeply laid neural highways lingering in his brain—so much so that his drinking routine became automatic or "hardwired." As Harold walked by the bar, his brain's pathway for drinking took over, and he found himself sitting at the bar and drinking before he could think consciously and critically about the situation he was putting himself in. This kind of hardwiring is a normal, biological process that can work for you or against you. In Harold's case, it worked against him.

Hardwiring certain behaviors can work to our advantage, especially when those behaviors allow us to perform regular activities with little to no effort. Consider driving a car. When we first learn to drive, we must concentrate and consciously choose when to press the gas and brake pedals, how hard to turn the wheel, and which gear to be in. Once we become experienced, however, we don't really think about those things anymore because they've become so routine. Only when something unexpected happens, like a car darting in front of us, do we rapidly shift into a conscious, decision-making process and slam our foot on the brakes.

We do all kinds of different activities, like driving, with so much frequency that our brains learn to perform them on autopilot. The scientific literature calls this "automaticity." For Harold, he'd walked past the bar so many times that the action itself triggered his automatic, programmed behavior.

I will explore triggers in greater depth in the next chapter, but the main idea to explore here is the role of repetition in creating automatic, "autopilot" thoughts and behaviors. Every repetition of an action increases the likelihood of the same action occurring in the future, so let's examine the concept of automaticity within the context of character development.

Shaping Personal Character

Neural networks with a high probability of activation manifest themselves in our expressions of character. In other words, our personal character emerges from our brain activity. And we can shape our character by harnessing the power of automaticity to ingrain positive, healthy habits and behaviors into our lives.

To shape our character through our habits, we must understand that whatever you do consistently becomes what you do automatically. This is likely a biological component that explains why people will persist in doing the very things they do not want to do. But this can change! The same brain mechanisms that get us into a mess can also help us get out of it.

We want right actions to come automatically instead of undesirable ones. That means we need to repeat actions that demonstrate the fruit of the Spirit—love, joy, peace, patience, kindness, goodness, faithfulness, gentleness, and self-control—so that they become entrenched in our brains. As we cultivate the fruit of the Spirit, our need to consciously direct ourselves toward moral actions lessens because we slowly embed them into our character until they become automatic, or a deeply furrowed path or superhighway.

Imagine you want to change your angry attitude toward your enemies. You understand this change won't happen all at once, so you start praying for them as the Bible says in Matthew 5:44: "Love your enemies and pray for those who persecute you" (NIV). It's arguably a small step toward your desired change, but loving actions like this, when performed repeatedly, influence neural systems. Those systems learn to support your loving actions, thereby improving their ability to fire. This repetition makes it more likely that you'll respond with loving actions in future circumstances. In short, your praying for enemies primes your brain to act godly toward them instead of choosing an ugly response.

Studies reinforcing the power of moral automaticity have focused on people deemed moral giants, or people who do the right thing at great personal cost or effort. Think Mother Theresa, Harriet Tubman, and Oskar Schindler. Surprisingly, when moral giants were asked why they chose to do the right thing despite the personal cost, they typically answered that they could not have done differently, assuming anyone else would have acted the same way.[10] They did not need to weigh the pros and cons of their decisions because doing the right thing came naturally to them. The possibility of making a different decision was often not even within their awareness.

As theologian Gregory Peterson said, "What studies of moral giants show is that the solution to weakness of will is not getting a stronger will, but rather achieving a set of mind that makes the language of willing either irrelevant or a special case, arising only in certain circumstances or for certain people."[11] To repeat, the solution to weakness of will is not developing a stronger will; the solution to weakness is developing righteous habits (a.k.a. automatic behaviors) so that "willing" and "choosing" are not even parts of the process.

> The solution to weakness of will is not developing a stronger will; the solution to weakness is developing righteous habits.

Doing the right thing is less about conscious reasoning than it is about establishing the proper automatic response. When acting lovingly becomes automatic and habitual, we are able to demonstrate love even in circumstances that would otherwise provoke negative responses. Anyone can become a moral giant with the right training.

Training to Forgive

On October 2, 2006, a gunman entered a one-room Amish school in Nickel Mines, Pennsylvania. He ordered the teachers and the boys to leave but held ten girls hostage. After tying up the girls, he explained that he was angry at God for the premature death of his own daughter. He then opened fire on the girls, killing five of them and critically wounding the others. As the police stormed the school, the man turned the gun on himself.

Within hours, the Amish community extended forgiveness to the shooter and his family. Members of the community gave flowers, food, and hugs to the gunman's widow. Half the people in attendance at the gunman's funeral were Amish, many of whom were family members of the slain girls. They even contributed to a fund for the gunman's family. Their forgiveness did not mean they weren't bearing profound pain and grief. They most certainly were. Yet they offered forgiveness despite their pain and grief.

The Amish community's swift and powerful act of forgiveness, both in word and in deed, after something so tragic stunned the world. In the month that followed, thousands of news stories and hundreds of thousands of websites featured Amish forgiveness.[12] Many of the reports focused on "saintliness" in a way that made the Amish community's forgiveness seem otherworldly or unattainable for the masses when, in reality, it was their community's upholding of a lifelong commitment to forgiveness that enabled them to absolve the gunman of his heinous act. Their forgiveness neurons were already strong from years of practicing it. Consequently, the reporters missed the opportunity to explain to the general public how practicing forgiveness as a lifestyle, like the Amish, could make such forgiveness possible and attainable within their own respective communities—provided they put in the work and apply it.[13]

For most people, forgiveness tends to come at the end of a long emotional journey. It's understandably difficult to forgive major offenses right out of the gate, especially if we haven't been training our forgiveness neurons. But we can train ourselves up in strengthening our forgiveness neurons, and that is a source of hope.

When you need to forgive a major offense, try not to beat yourself up over how long it's taking you and reframe your forgiveness as a journey. Still take your pain to God. Still pray that you are able to forgive. Pray to have the character traits of someone who forgives without delay. If God doesn't seem to answer you right away, be patient and give yourself grace.

Apply this idea in a completely different context: Should a novice runner beat herself up because she's not yet able to finish a marathon? Of course not. Forgiveness requires mental and emotional processing and practice. We can begin this practice by setting aside a big offense and focusing first on smaller ones. After all, how can we expect to forgive big things if we haven't practiced forgiving small things? Practice forgiveness in short sprints—extend it to the reckless driver, the rude customer, or, in my case, my kid who finds culinary delights between couch cushions.

Learning to forgive major offenses is a long-term goal, a marathon that we must work toward, to continue our running metaphor. But encouragement waits at each mile marker as we become one step closer to our goal. And if you don't have a major offense on your plate now, count yourself blessed but continue to train daily. That way, when a major offense inevitably occurs, you readily extend forgiveness because you've trained your brain to automatically respond with grace.

To be clear, extending forgiveness does not require you to remain buddies with an offender. A primary text on forgiveness is found in Matthew 18:21–35, where Jesus tells Peter there is no limit to the number of times Peter should forgive someone. But this does not mean that you're expected to continually put up with someone else's bad behavior or abuse. Anyone who supports that notion misunderstands the context of those particular verses entirely.

Matthew 18:15–18, which precedes the verses on extending forgiveness, provides the steps for reconciliation. This passage first instructs us to confront our offender privately. If the offender does not acknowledge their fault when confronted, then confront them with a few other witnesses. If that doesn't work, then confront them publicly. If the person still refuses to accept responsibility and correct their behavior, then yes, we still forgive them, but we are also allowed to kick them to the curb. Or as the Bible says, "Treat that person as a pagan or a corrupt tax collector" (Matthew 18:17 NLT).

If a person says to you something along the lines of, "Biblically speaking, you have to forgive me and allow me back into your life and confidence. And when I reoffend, we'll repeat this process," remember that you have biblical authority that says otherwise. You are to forgive, but you don't have to tolerate their behavior and suffer as their perpetual victim. Let them know that if they want to have a relationship with you, then they must change their behavior. List for them the changes that need to be made and stick to your established boundaries.

I witnessed a beautiful transformation in the relationship between a client and his estranged adult daughter, who established hard boundaries as a condition to resurrecting their relationship. When she was a young girl, he had used her as a human shield during a shootout with the FBI and then abandoned her after receiving a twenty-year prison sentence. After his release and without warning, he showed up at her door while high on heroin, begging her to forgive him and let him live with her.

This woman and I were acquaintances from church, so she called me for help. We got her father into rehabilitation, and she refused to have contact with him until she saw that he truly was a changed person. Inspiringly, he did change, and they rebuilt their relationship, but it took a long time for him to prove himself a changed man. And if he hadn't changed, his daughter would have been perfectly justified in saying, "I forgive you but will not have a relationship with you."

Failure and Perseverance

When I was much younger, I attended a church in which some people demonstrated their rigorous spiritual discipline as if it were a badge of honor.

"I wake up at six in the morning every day to pray," someone would say.

"Well, I get up at five," another person would add.

"I pray for two hours."

"I pray for three."

I sleep in as long as I can, I'd think to myself. *I pray at night, but I often fall asleep mid-prayer. God gets my drool just as often as he gets my requests.* My prayer life obviously needed improvement, but the pressure to wake up at four in the morning and pray for hours at a time was unrealistic and discouraging.

When it comes to spiritual discipline, it seems that some churches expect people to go from zero to sixty. But going zero to sixty often leads to a crash. Most prayer novices cannot metamorphosize into prayer warriors overnight, just as sedentary people cannot run a marathon without incremental training. The people at my former church and their testimonies of lengthy prayer sessions were driving away new believers who felt they were expected to keep up and not fail or fall short.

The hard truth is that making any kind of change almost always includes some degree of failure. Most clients at the long-term, residential rehab program I worked at had attended five, seven, or even twelve different rehabilitation programs before ours. Some clients were in their second stay with us, having failed their first time around. While I did not track hard numbers, it was my observation that returning clients fared better than those on their first try.

> Any kind of change almost always includes some degree of failure.

How many times *does* it take for sobriety to stick? Unfortunately, we have no specific answer. There isn't a universal definition or plan for success because it's subjective. A program may boast a 90 percent success rate but measure success as one day of sobriety. Another program might report a 60 percent success rate and label success as program completion—without tracking a client's post-program activity. Another might claim 30 percent, but their criteria require a person to not only remain sober for a year post-graduation but to also secure gainful employment.

But what about the person who drank excessively every day before checking into rehab, then graduated from the program and remained sober for a year before slipping up one Saturday night? What if that same person woke up the following Sunday morning, applied the coping skills they learned in rehab, utilized resources for support, and claimed another year of sobriety? Are they a failure? Some programs would say yes. Personally, I think the ability to stand back up after a fall is what makes us a success.

> The ability to stand back up after a fall is what makes us a success.

Standing back up after a fall of any kind is hard. It reminds me of an interesting observation an employee of a gaming company once shared with me. Many games on phones and computers offer a daily reward for playing. What the employee noted was that a new player who missed a couple days of rewards would, in all likelihood, continue to play the game. But a long-term player who missed several days of rewards was not likely to return. I immediately applied this same phenomenon to recovering addicts.

When a newly sober person relapses, they're usually able to get back on their feet quickly. They didn't lose much because they hadn't gained much. Conversely, when a person with long-term sobriety relapses, they may very well stay relapsed for a while. They'll throw in the towel and declare their sober time lost down the drain. The loss feels too big and the disappointment too painful.

Addicts who relapse don't realize that they didn't lose all that sober time because their brain hasn't returned to its former shape. At least not yet. All of their hard work is still right there inside their head. But the longer they stay down, the more their superhighway of sobriety is demolished and the more their path of addiction is cemented.

The same holds true for anyone making a change in their life. A pastor once admitted that it took him more than thirty years to stop being a mean person. There were stretches of time when he would treat others with kindness, but life would inevitably throw him a curveball that brought out the angry monster in him. He would get in a person's face and yell, and whenever this happened, he'd later think to himself, *I am just a mean person. That's who I am. Why fight it?* Nevertheless, he persevered in his commitment to change and never threw in the towel, and he managed to put that monster to rest.

Developing Spiritual Discipline

To return to prayer as an example of spiritual discipline, we sometimes forget that prayer is a learned skill and one that improves with practice. We can't simply tell someone that prayer is like talking to a friend and then suddenly expect them to start having hours-long conversations with God. And let's be honest. A lot of the time, prayer does not feel like talking to a friend. With a friend, we have someone to engage in conversation with. But if we haven't learned to listen for the still, small voice of God, prayer can seem like we're casting words into a void.

Just like marathon runners need proper coaching to advance from short-distance jogs to long-distance runs, people need both time and training to successfully develop their spiritual disciplines. They need to start small and work up to more complex spiritual practices. We also need to understand the athlete as an individual. Every athlete is different, and their training needs are different.

For example, I would never counsel clients with attention deficit hyperactivity disorder (ADHD) to sit and pray for long stretches of time. Their lack of success would discourage them, and their motivation to foster an active prayer life would fall away. Instead, I tell them to pray in short snippets throughout the day—a minute or two here and there. Or I might encourage them to structure their prayer times so that sometime before lunch, they give thanks. Between lunch and dinner, they make personal requests. Before bed, they make requests for others.

By the end of the day, this person with ADHD may have cumulatively prayed more minutes than the person who prayed all at once. But by practicing their mini prayers (and really, they're not mini; a prayer is a prayer) throughout the day, they are well on their way to living the command to "pray without ceasing" (1 Thessalonians 5:17 NASB).

Like prayer, knowing how to read the Bible is also a skill that develops over time. We tell people to read their Bible, and if or when they struggle to understand it, we suggest trying a different translation, as if the sole issue is the complexity of the wording. They may indeed benefit from a different translation, but they also might need training. When people from other religions attend my Bible study, I usually have to begin by explaining what the New and Old Testaments are, why there are multiple books (not just names of new chapters), where the texts came from, and how those funny numbers all over the pages work.

True discipleship offers patience to people and their shortcomings. And it's up to us as fellow believers to encourage and uplift them as they strengthen their spiritual practices. We can assure new believers that with time and effort, the Bible will make more sense to them. Celebrate their progress and growth when they manage to pray for five solid minutes for the first time. Teach them how to listen for God's voice. Teach them who God is so that the idea of prayerful conversation with him draws them in.

Praying Forward

We often pray directly for whatever it is that we want to change, as if we could will God into making it happen (remember the failure of willpower?). *God, take away this anger…God, help me with this craving for alcohol…God, why am I so weak?* With the way the brain works, however, we might be strengthening our anger, craving, or weakness in the very way that we're trying to pray it away. So what is the alternative? Don't pray backward. Pray forward!

God, take away this anger that I feel toward my coworker is a backward prayer. The forward prayer is *God, I pray for a spirit of peace. I pray for the ability to react to this person with kindness.* Or, to use a prayer from my own life, *I pray that I will respond in graceful firmness when my children whine* instead of *I pray that I won't be snippy and exasperated.*

If the focus of my prayer is snippiness and exasperation, then I risk strengthening those negative responses in my brain even though I don't want to. Later, when my kids start to whine, out comes a harsh remark quickly followed by intense parental guilt. That's why I pray for how I *want* to react instead—because I'm more likely to react in that way. Pray less about what you are running from and more about what you are running toward.

> Pray less about what you are running from and more about what you are running toward.

The Bible cautions against looking back, and it is not too much of a stretch to apply that to one's prayer life. A well-known story about the dangers of looking back is the story of Lot's wife in Genesis 19. Lot and his family were fleeing the destruction of their city, and when his wife turned to look back at the destruction, she turned into a pillar of salt. The Bible doesn't tell us why she looked back. Regret? Curiosity? Melancholy? Perhaps the natural desire to rubberneck at the proverbial car wreck? Ultimately, it doesn't matter why she looked back. What matters is the lesson of looking forward.

Philippians 3:13 tells us to forget what is behind and strain toward what is ahead. Isaiah 43:18–19 tells us not to remember the former things nor consider the things of old because God is doing a new thing. Let's pray for these new things so that our brain grows toward them, making these positive changes more likely to occur as we become more likely to act in ways to achieve them.

Pray for strength and courage instead of praying for God to take away your weakness, whatever it may be. Pray for the fruit of the Spirit, and not just in a general sense but specifically how you want to exhibit them. Take it a step further by specifying the situations in which you want to demonstrate the fruit of the Spirit. Your mind will prime itself to do precisely that.

Dark Night of the Soul

For a long time, the medically recommended treatment for a person with a traumatic brain injury was to attend physical therapy until he or she no longer showed signs of improvement. The assumption was that the patient had reached their maximum potential for recovery once hitting this first plateau, and the focus of therapy would then shift to symptom management.

However, research has since shown that a person who continues therapy during times of plateau will often later experience a surge of improvement, followed by another plateau, then another period of improvement.[14] For that reason, the current assumption is that recovery is nonlinear; it's normal for these patients to experience times of great progress and times of regression.

After successfully practicing something for a brief period of time, we might conclude that improvement comes relatively easily. And in some ways, we'd be right because we are, in fact, strengthening existing synaptic connections. But then it might feel like we plateau or backslide because maintaining improvement and making it permanent requires the slow, steady work of forging new brain connections. Our neurons are hard at work consolidating recent growth and slowly establishing the connections required for the next phase of progress.

If you haven't already heard the phrase "dark night of the soul," it's a term for a spiritual crisis in which a believer feels unable to grow or that God is absent. What we want to remember during dark nights or periods of dark nights is that this uncomfortable and discouraging phase could very well be our brain's way of catching up and preparing for the next phase, the next leap in our faith journey. Maybe that leap will be a new experience in sensing God, or a positive shift in our character, a deepening of our spiritual disciplines, a new motivation for service, or a new life direction. Get excited about your next leap!

Summary

The first principle to understand about personal change is that your brain is capable of it thanks to neuroplasticity. Your brain changes through the activities it performs, both in thought and in deed, so the habits you think or perform most often create neural pathways in your brain, making those same habits more likely to happen. What you think and do today not only changes your brain but also impacts what you think and do in the future. Neglected brain pathways and the habits they lead to, on the other hand, fade away. In short, "use it or lose it."

> What you think and do today not only changes your brain but also impacts what you think and do in the future.

Second, in understanding how you can modify these pathways in your brain, you become equipped to take the necessary steps to deliberately neglect the paths that lead to unwanted thoughts and behaviors and build up the paths toward the thoughts and behaviors you *do* want. Brain traffic wants to take the easiest, fastest routes, so you must consciously redirect your thoughts in the direction you want them to go.

Remember that the willpower approach to change tends to make things worse. By attempting to will your way out of a bad habit, you actually strengthen the very habit you seek to change. Learn to redirect your focus toward something positive.

Rather than feeling discouraged or giving up when your brain traffic inevitably steers off course, give yourself grace. Setbacks are part of the hard work. And with every victory, even the seemingly trivial ones, your brain reroutes you in the direction of future success. In time, right action and right thought become your automatic responses because they've become natural expressions of your character.

Just like brain change is a gradual process, your spiritual discipline is its own kind of journey too. It takes time and effort to develop your practices, such as prayer, forgiveness, or growing in the fruit of the Spirit. Treat yourself and others with grace during times of growth and change so that we all grow stronger together. True discipleship offers patience to people and their shortcomings. It's up to us as fellow believers to encourage and uplift each other as we strengthen our spiritual practices.

Lastly, consider the following questions. What would it look like if you approached spiritual training like physical training? What if you intentionally exercise weak muscles? And as a church, what would it look like to adopt an incremental approach to teaching spiritual disciplines to the congregation?

Reflect

1. Since your brain is shaped by what you think and do, map out your time. Draw a circle on a piece of paper and divide it into sections proportionate to the amount of time you spend on the responsibilities, activities, and thoughts you're most devoted to.

    Sections could include things like your job, your kids, your prayer life, or your frequently recurring emotions, such as anxiety or anger. If you estimate that you spend 25 percent of your time on your job, for example, dedicate a quarter of the circle to it.

Once your circle is fully sectioned out, analyze it. Which aspect of your life is getting the most amount of your time? Which is getting the least? What do you want to change about your brain map?

2. What have you been working to overcome through sheer willpower yet finding limited success with? What thoughts or activities can you redirect yourself toward instead of relying on willpower?

3. Think about your primary, recurring prayer requests and the language you use for them. Are you praying backward or forward? If you are praying backward, how can you rephrase your prayers so that you're praying forward instead?

4. Evaluate your brain pathways: Do they inspire righteousness and faithfulness or those that lead to temptation or negativity? Which pathways do you want to fire faster in your daily encounters?

5. Name two small steps you will take to train up and strengthen pathways related to your spiritual life.

Chapter 3

Neurons that Fire Together, Wire Together: "Why Did I Do That?"

Not long after starting my work at the rehabilitation center, I stumbled upon a riddle of sorts. Every two weeks, a small population of residents at the center would experience a strong, powerful drug craving. They were typically fine otherwise, but when day fourteen rolled around, they became cranky, made poor behavioral decisions, and were generally a mess. It was like clockwork. What was going on?

The answer to the craving riddle can be found in the brain's formation of connections. In the last chapter, we talked about the ways in which neurons strengthen or weaken depending on the frequency with which they're used and the neural pathways they create. If we practice kindness often, then our ability to show kindness becomes a habit and ingrained in our character. If we lie frequently, then lying becomes second nature. We can see why it's important to cultivate the good stuff and weaken the bad stuff.

Neural Linking

In addition to strengthening and weakening the neurons them-selves, neurons also forge connections to each other based on their frequency of use. When two neurons activate at the same time, the connection between them strengthens. And if those two neurons repeatedly activate together at the same time, they become functionally linked, such that activity in one facilitates activation of the other.[15] They form a knot, so to speak, almost operating as a single unit. And this not only occurs between two neurons but also entire groups of neurons. Neurobiologist Carla Shatz summarizes this mechanism in a pithy statement, often quoted in neuroscience and popular science writings: "Neurons that fire together, wire together."[16]

Think of a traffic light. Our neurons have formed connec-tions that link colors with actions: green means go, red means stop, and yellow means slow down (or go faster depending on your driving habits). We see a red light, which activates our response to hit the brakes.

Brain knots can have profound implications on our lives. I'll give you a personal example. At one point in our relationship, my wife and I were dating long distance. She was in seminary, and I was working several states away. During a phone call, she asked if she could borrow my book of John Wesley's sermons for an upcoming class. "Of course," I said. While wrapping up the book to mail it to her, I thought it would be romantic to spray a little bit of my cologne in the package so that when she opened it, she would smell it and think of me.

The next time we met in person and hugged, however, she said, "Ugh! You need to get rid of that cologne. When I hug you all I can think of is John Wesley." A semester of her working with the book and the scent of my cologne permeating its pages had forged a new link in her brain. Those scent neurons formerly associated with me were now associated with a 1700s pastor and theologian, much to my dismay. I promptly threw away my cologne, and it was back to the scent neuron drawing board for me.

In another example, I was talking to a woman who could not pray the rosary without feeling upset and distressed. After much reflection, she remembered that her mother made the children in their family pray the rosary as punishment every time they misbehaved. The woman's brain had linked prayer with feelings of punishment, creating an impediment to her prayer life even though she could not readily remember the context in which the link was established in the first place.

Similarly, I learned of a youth group leader who punished misbehaving teens by forcing them to read the book of Chronicles in the Bible. I almost leaped out of my seat to call the guy because he was linking feelings of punishment with reading the Bible. These kids might consciously forget this youth group experience, but the negative neural connection they've made between punishment and reading the Bible could very well persist into adulthood. They won't want to read the Bible later in life and might not even know why.

Consider the dejected man who once sat in my office as I perused his arrest record. I looked at him incredulously before asking, "Seven accounts of firebombing? Seriously?"

He stared at me blankly. "Yeah, but that's just how people break up. You set their car on fire," he replied. "Haven't you ever broken up with someone before?" This man's brain had somehow linked the ending of a romantic relationship with firebombing an ex's vehicle.

The power of neural linking cannot be underestimated. Biologist Gregory Gerdeman summarizes studies on drug addiction that illustrate its power. Not only does he explain how the desire for the euphoria (or "high") that drugs produce influences a person's addiction, but he also explains how the actions and rituals required to obtain the drug also link to the high. In short, feelings of pleasure motivate the early stages of addiction, but the behavioral practices and habits that addicts develop in securing the drug drive the later stages of their addiction.

Gerdeman describes the following pathway. Dopamine neurons, which produce the high, first fire in association with the use of the drug. That is, a person takes the drug and experiences the high, and then their brain links the drug with feelings of pleasure. If that person continues to use that drug, then they probably have to go through the same motions to acquire and use it, whether that's meeting the same dealer, buying the same brand of alcohol, or preparing the drug the same way they always do. By repeating these ritualistic motions, the brain links the reward or high with the rituals, so much so that longer-term addicts may experience the high during the rituals before even consuming the drug.[17]

Neural links can also affect your relationship with God. A person with a fraught or absent relationship with their father may struggle or feel uncomfortable with the concept of God as a heavenly Father. Their preexisting, negative associations with a father transfer to their perception of God, leaving them to wrestle with conflicting feelings and ideas or an inability to feel God as love. Many of my clients had problematic relationships with their fathers and faced this very challenge, so I taught them alternative ways to consider him. For example, I'd tell them to see God as their Shepherd and to root their relationship with him in Psalm 23, or I'd suggest they see him as their Redeemer since the Bible has many examples of God's redemption, or to simply consider him a friend.[18]

By recognizing and understanding the neural links we forge in our brains (and the links imposed on us by others), we become aware of our emotional roadblocks. We're then able to identify how those roadblocks trigger unwanted behavioral patterns so that we can overcome them.

> By recognizing and understanding the neural links we forge in our brains (and the links imposed on us by others), we become aware of our emotional roadblocks.

Triggers

When unrelated neurons forge a link as a result of repeated, associated activities, we create a triggering effect in our brain. That is, our behaviors link with specific stimuli, such as people, places, things, or emotions. As a result, these stimuli become triggers eliciting emotions, behaviors, and even memories. The stimulus and the response share a neural link, so whenever one of the neurons in the shared link fires, the neuron on the other side of the link fires too.

Remember Harold from the previous chapter? He walked past the bar he used to frequent and found himself drinking before he knew it. The bar was the stimuli, which his brain linked with a series of subsequent behaviors: opening the door, stepping inside, finding a seat at the bar, and ordering a drink. Had he understood that the neurons in his brain had linked the bar with drinking, he could have taken a different route and avoided his trigger: seeing the bar.

To return to the riddle from the beginning of this chapter, what neural link was responsible for triggering the intense cravings the recovering addicts experienced at the rehab center every two weeks? Rest assured we cracked the code, but in order to understand it, we first must understand functioning addicts. Functioning addicts are people who manage to maintain a job and usually some semblance of a social life in the midst of their addiction. Others may not even notice that a person is a functioning addict because his or her life appears normal from the outside.

Prior to entering rehab, the functioning addicts were paid every two weeks by their employers. Once paid, they used those funds to buy their drug of choice. Their internal clocks linked with their drug use, resulting in severe cravings every two weeks, and their minds and bodies reacted accordingly—even months into sobriety.

In another story, a few addicts related to me that while they enjoyed contemporary church services, they also struggled whenever they were physically inside the church. The addicts with this particular struggle often came from rock and roll culture and attributed their addictions to their former lifestyle. And it turned out that the musical styles and sounds they heard in contemporary church venues were too similar to the musical styles and sounds associated with their past, thereby triggering unpleasant or destructive thoughts and feelings.

When these addicts switched churches to those with different styles of music, their spiritual growth typically improved. This is not to disparage contemporary worship music—at all. People can experience these same triggering responses to traditional hymns. It all depends on how a person's past experiences shaped their brain.

We all have highly complex, unique triggers, and they're not always bad. I've already mentioned some common ones, like the colors of a stoplight triggering certain driving behaviors. Certain foods are also commonly associated with feelings of comfort, and certain songs can trigger positive or negative memories and feelings. Calendar dates can trigger joy: birthdays, anniversaries, or Christmas. Other dates can trigger sadness, like a deceased loved one's birthday. The good news is that we can rewire our neural links.

The good news is that we can rewire our neural links.

Rewiring Neural Links

The solution to rewiring a neural link is twofold: awareness and preparation. To use the functioning addicts with the cravings every two weeks as an example, they first needed to become aware of the neural link between their internal clock and their craving. Then they had to prepare themselves for the two-week mark by planning to be in a safe place with safe people. This prevented the craving from derailing their recovery.

My former client, Andy, lends a perfect illustration of what it looks like to rewire a neural link. One day, a resident at the rehab center insulted Andy, so Andy picked up a large rock and wound back his arm, preparing to hurl it square into the resident's face. Everyone froze. The supervisor calmly told Andy to put down the rock, and we could see Andy struggle to decide what to do next.

It was as if a cartoon devil and angel appeared on each of Andy's shoulders, the devil whispering, "Throw it, he deserves it!" and the angel asserting, "Put it down! You don't want to be expelled, do you?" Andy slowly lowered his hand and let the rock fall to the ground. We all breathed a sigh of relief.

Later in my office, Andy said, "I feel lousy for dropping the rock. I feel like less of a man for not standing up for myself. If I did the right thing, then why do I feel so bad about it?"

"You feel bad because you used to link violent reactions with manliness and standing up for yourself," I explained. "You had linked backing down, letting something go, and forgiving others with being weak or taken advantage of and having low self-respect. So you used violence to maintain your positive self-concept."

I continued to praise Andy for dropping the rock and assured him that he had taken a tremendous step forward. His quandary of how to respond to the insult demonstrated that he was developing an awareness of his triggers. He was starting to rewire positive emotions with nonviolent responses to confrontation.

The staff at the rehab center also met to figure out how we could structure Andy's work program so that he could continue to practice these healthy, positive responses as we continued to guide him. As one of our counselors once said, "We pack as many problems into one hundred acres as possible," meaning that our clients had to learn to face their problems in a supervised environment in order to learn how to respond to them appropriately in other environments.

We have to learn to respond to hard things in positive ways to establish positive neural links. Avoiding or taking a break from our problems and emotions does not serve us. We must expose ourselves to challenging experiences so that we can train ourselves to react and behave in the ways we want and to experience the emotions we want.

> We have to learn to respond to hard things in positive ways to establish positive neural links.

Creating a New Worldview

As we've seen in the stories I've shared thus far, each person's brain uniquely links together various emotions, thoughts, and behaviors, and rewiring those neural links is hard work. What further complicates this work are our past experiences. They color what we see and remember, and we tend to only see whatever our past has trained us to see.

> We tend to only see whatever our past has trained us to see.

Psychologist Carol Izard describes this coloring effect as "affective-cognitive schemas," where emotions, cognition, and behaviors enhance and modify one another through mutual feedback.[19] A schema itself describes a mental pattern or framework that organizes information about the world. Schemas use our existing knowledge and experiences to help us anticipate what to expect in a situation or an event. A schema for a grocery store, for example, would likely include aisles with shelves of food, shopping carts, and cash registers.

Assemblies of strengthened neural connections make up schemas, and they tend to activate as units in response to particular stimuli. Entire ensembles, or schemas, of perception, emotion, and behavior can link together. That's a lot of science-y language, so I'll share an example.

I asked a client named Tom to imagine receiving a decent amount of money. "What is the first thing you're going to do with it?" I asked him.

"Prostitutes and crack."

Oh, dear. Here was a neural link we needed to address. More specifically, we needed to unlink his concept of money from harmful behaviors and relink it with something different, preferably something positive.

Pursuing this track, I added, "What about saving up for a place to stay or to buy something you need?"

"No way," Tom said. "If you hold on to your money, either a debt collector will grab it, or someone will steal it. Whenever you get money, you gotta spend it all right away."

Tom's response revealed his entire worldview, his schema, about money. His life experience conditioned him to believe that saving money was a bad idea because it would inevitably be taken from him.

Like Tom's, our worldviews are made up of multiple schemas, and they impact not only how we process our thoughts and emotions but also how we react with our behavior. I'll share a personal example that reflects how schemas affect what we see and do.

I struck up a conversation with a homeless man one night a few days before Christmas. He was thirsty and wanted water, so I drove him around, stopping the car at various establishments. He would go inside and quickly emerge defeated by employees who balked at his scruffy appearance. We faced considerable difficulty, but we eventually found a restaurant (preparing to close) where a server gave him a glass from their kitchen.

When I finally got home and shared the night's ordeal with my wife, she asked, "Why didn't you just go into one of those places and get the water for him yourself?"

Dumbstruck, I realized that option had never even occurred to me. I was employed by a nonprofit that helped the homeless, so I always turned to and worked within organizations to assist homeless people. My methods were to connect homeless people with social systems and resources and equip them to take action for themselves. That was the emotional, cognitive, and behavioral schema in my brain.

So when a homeless man sat in my car and asked for water, I approached his need in the same manner: I encouraged him to obtain water using the resources I made available to him. I had no trouble talking to him about his personal problems, but when it came to water, I never thought of getting it for him myself.

We see the world not as it is but as we are. Or as psychologist Abraham Maslow summarizes it, "If you become highly skilled at using a hammer, you see every problem as a nail."[20] To quote philosopher Abraham Kaplan's more humorous statement, "Give a small boy a hammer, and he will find everything he encounters needs pounding"[21]—a statement well illustrated the day my then two-year-old ran through the living room, hammer in hand, screaming, "Look what I found! Now I can bam things!"

We see the world not as it is but as we are.

Part of what makes personal change so difficult is that we tend to only notice information that fits into our existing schemas. Even when we receive contradictory information, we might not even register it, ignoring or forgetting it entirely.[22] We sometimes go so far as to reinterpret information and alter our memories to fit our existing schema. Take people with negative self-esteem for example. They tend to remember negative information about themselves, discount positive information, and create a bias in their memory to support their negative outlook.[23] This is why compliments just don't seem to stick with them. They hear a compliment, but because they don't believe it to be true, they dismiss or forget the compliment entirely.

As I mentioned in the introduction, some brain pathways are so strong and so deep that we cannot change them ourselves, particularly those paths that prevent us from accepting contradictory information. It begs the question: If our dominant brain pathways and schemas blind us, how can we train ourselves to make the changes we wish to see?

Training Behaviors, Emotions, and Morals

As I mentioned earlier in the book, it's critical that we establish a support system when making a change. We need people to cheer us on and praise our good decisions to help us wire good feelings *to* those good decisions. Counselors, small groups, pastors, and good friends all fit the bill. We also need them to relay feedback and repeat information to us until we start to create new links in our brain. And if we want them to be open and honest about their feedback, we need to grant them permission to stage interventions with us.

> We need people to cheer us on and praise our good decisions to help us wire good feelings *to* those good decisions.

Interventions are not just for people in denial of substance abuse problems, and they don't have to be intense confrontations either. They can be simple offerings of constructive feedback, and they guide us in making course corrections, big and small. I remember when my wife and a friend of mine staged an intervention with me. They said my emails were starting to sound too formal, stiff, and business-like. In my busyness and motivation to get things done, I was coming across unfriendly and impersonal. I hadn't even noticed that my tone had shifted, but I accepted the feedback and asked my wife if she would "police" my tone in a few of my upcoming emails. She proofread a few of them until they read better, and then I was able to prioritize friendliness over efficiency again. I like to think that this small intervention probably helped benefit a few friendships.

Second, we need to train our emotions. Many people think our emotions are automatic; they happen to a person, and that person has little control over them. John Wesley, the eighteenth-century theologian who stole my cologne, believed people were responsible for their emotions but was not ignorant of the fact that emotions arise uncontrollably in response to an experience.

Wesley classified two types of emotions: affections and tempers. Affections are temporary feelings that emerge in response to experiences, situations, and objects. That is, we experience feelings, but we are not guilty, bad, or responsible for having experienced them. What we are responsible for is what we *do* with those feelings. If someone cuts ahead of us in line, of course we're going to be annoyed, and that's okay. What matters, and what we're responsible for according to Wesley, is how we react to feeling annoyed. Do we politely remind the budger of the line behind them, or do we call them a jerk and thumb them to the back of the line?

Tempers, on the other hand, are emotions we allow ourselves to feel again and again in response to experiences, situations, and objects. These emotions become habits, shaping not only our temper but also defining our character. And unlike affections, Wesley says we are responsible for our tempers. If we heatedly confront every person who cuts ahead of us in line, then we've allowed ourselves to become aggressive, confrontational people, and we're on the hook for that.

Psychologist John Bargh explains this in another way, distinguishing emotions from moods. He states that emotions may be immediate responses to the environment, but moods are of lesser intensity and longer duration. Bargh also states that intentional thought can play a role in the development of our emotional responses. Thinking positive thoughts, for example, can reduce feelings of pressure or stress in situations conducive to those feelings, and by practicing positive thoughts, we can change our automatic emotional responses over time.[24]

> By practicing positive thoughts, we can change our automatic emotional responses over time.

Returning to Wesley, he further classifies tempers as holy or unholy, meaning beneficial to moral growth or not beneficial. Although unholy tempers tend to operate unconsciously, we are nevertheless responsible for healing them. The ultimate goal, and a central part of Christian growth, is to transform unholy tempers into holy ones. Then, once our new holy tempers become habits, holy actions will naturally flow from our holy dispositions.

How do we train temporary feelings into holy tempers? Wesley said this training is primarily accomplished by placing ourselves in situations in which we are guaranteed to experience a particular feeling and then intentionally replicating those situations to train the desired emotional feeling into a habit. Sound familiar? This was exactly how we approached emotional and behavioral change with addicts like Andy at the rehab center.

To illustrate the training of a holy temper, Wesley often used the example of our love for God and our love for others. That is, our love for others grows in response to our experience of God's love, and God's love is often mediated through others in community.

Modern scientific theories on emotion also hint at how we can train our emotions. These theories assign multiple parts to an emotional experience: the feeling that arises, the context surrounding our feeling, how we think about the feeling, and how we act because of it.[25] Each part influences the others to produce the cumulative emotional experience. And if we change one part, we can often change the emotion as a whole.[26]

It should also be understood that emotions play a significant role in our moral training and development. If we want a life lived in accordance with morality, it requires us to continually act upon our beliefs or values.[27] That means we first have to train our emotions so that our reactions *to* those emotions reflect our morals. Our moral development regresses if we consistently allow ourselves to fall short of our own moral expectations.

Most of us can probably agree that it sometimes seems like people with looser morals have more fun and fewer struggles, leaving us resentful of our choice to live morally. But this need not be the case. Leading a moral life does not have to be an emotional struggle. In fact, the Bible assures us that we can find joy in living morally.

The beatitudes in Matthew 5 are often described as "be happy" attitudes, as they bless those who are humble and merciful and "whose hearts are pure" (v. 8). Galatians 5 asserts that the Holy Spirit will produce the fruit of joy if we let the Spirit, instead of our sinful nature, guide our lives. Philippians 4:4 talks about rejoicing in the Lord, and many of the psalms are full of joy. Training our emotions, behaviors, and morals to reflect our faith enables us to experience true biblical joy.

One common theme among these verses is focus. The focus of each beatitude, for example, is what makes a person blessed. We need to focus on those reasons when things are tough. The focus of the Psalms as it relates to joy is the importance of recognizing God's character, goodness, the beauty of his creation, and how he has come through for us in the past. First Thessalonians 5:11 and Hebrews 10:24–25 focus on the need to encourage one another, and we've talked at length about the importance of having a support system when making a life change.

It's true that Psalm 73 talks about envying those who lead immoral lives, but then the psalmist repents of this attitude, shifting his focus instead to God and the long-term results of different life choices. Do we focus on the short-term gains someone might enjoy from wild living, or are we mindful of the more problematic long-term consequences they might face?

When we choose to focus on the joyful aspects of moral actions, we link that joy to the actions themselves. When we choose moral actions and are encouraged by others for those actions, we link the positive feelings from receiving encouragement with those moral actions too.

Emotional Reframing

When we're training our emotions, it is important to note that previous emotional states impact new emotional states. For example, if I like a person and then they insult me, the feeling I experience upon being insulted by them will differ from the feeling I experience if I were insulted by someone I dislike. I may initially feel angry at the insult, but if I reflect and determine it was meant as a joke, then the initial anger may morph into an entirely different emotion, like relief.

This example shows how we can modify our emotional responses by processing context. Like Wesley said, we may not be able to control an initial feeling, but we can control how we process and react to a situation both during and after. In doing so, we reframe our internal and external responses.

> We may not be able to control an initial feeling,
> but we can control how we process and react to a
> situation both during and after.

I practice emotional reframing with my kids by playing a game with them that I like to call "Reasons Why." When we're together and we see a person do something unkind or wrong, I pose to my kids the following question: "Can you think of reasons why this person might have done that?"

A classic example we've run into is someone cutting us off in traffic. "Why might that driver have made that decision?" I ask. And then my kids come up with possible explanations without blaming the offender for being a bad driver or a bad person. Rather, I challenge them to consider reasons why the driver might have made their choice. Maybe they were running late, or rushing to handle a personal emergency, or their kid was pitching a fit in the backseat, making it difficult for the driver to focus on the road.

Sometimes we do something wrong and explain or blame our error on factors outside of our control, but then, when someone else does something wrong, we blame it on their character. Psychologists call this phenomenon the "misattribution error." The "Reasons Why" game counters the misattribution error by training kids to be merciful and forgiving. And this game isn't limited to kids; adults can play and grow from it too.

We've learned how a previous emotional state can impact a new one. The reverse is also true; our response can impact our initial feeling. Let's use Andy's experience of wanting to hurl a rock into the face of his fellow resident for having insulted him. If Andy had thrown the rock, it probably would have felt good to him, like justice was served. His response in throwing the rock would then reframe his initial feeling of anger into one of satisfaction, thereby reinforcing a violent response. This had been Andy's past training—to feel good about hurting someone who hurt him, and it explains why he felt bad for not throwing the rock.

If we practice emotional reframing enough over time, we forge positive neural links and pathways. The emotional responses we develop from this reframing become so routinized and automatic that we bypass the conscious appraisal state of assigning blame entirely. Instead, it becomes our second nature to consider other explanations—not only for our own choices and behaviors but also the choices and behaviors of others. This ability to reframe our emotions becomes particularly helpful when it comes to forgiving others.

Reframing and Forgiveness

Have you ever forgiven someone but still felt angry afterward? Who hasn't? It's natural to feel angry when someone does something hurtful to us. And let's face it, when someone hurts us, it's easy to replay the hurtful event in our mind, and we grow angrier with every repetition. Soon it becomes difficult *not* to replay it.

Anger practiced regularly can strengthen anger pathways in the brain and, consequently, shape your character into an angry one. Along with growing stronger, the anger neurons start to link with neurons associated with the offender. The more we think about the person who offended us, the angrier we feel. It's like having a brain knot that ties the offender to our anger. And the longer we let that knot live inside our brain, the stronger and tighter the knot becomes. In this way, we see how anger makes forgiveness a difficult and complicated undertaking.

It should also be understood that anger in and of itself isn't necessarily wrong or bad. In fact, we see plenty of anger in the Bible. Paul tells us in Ephesians 4:26 to be angry but not to sin. In John chapter 2, Jesus became so angry with people selling livestock and exchanging money inside the temple that he flipped over their tables and drove them out with a whip (vv. 13–16). He had a temple tantrum, so to speak. Anger—in the right place, at the right time, for the right reason, and in the right amount— reveals what is important to us. And it can be a powerful force that spurs people into action.

Like we said in Chapter 2, forgiveness is a journey. If we want to move through the journey quickly and effectively, then we must not only train our forgiveness neurons, but we must also build strong neural pathways for those neurons. We do this by continually, consciously reminding ourselves of the importance of forgiveness and by practicing it. We must unlink the pathway in our brain connecting our anger with the offender by reminding ourselves (potentially for a lengthy period of time) that we have chosen to forgive them. We also need to introduce new, positive emotions. This helps dissolve the anger brain knot and replace it with a healthier, more positive association.

Prayer can help us forge new brain associations with people too. Matthew 5:44 says to "pray for those who persecute you" (NASB), not "God help that no good person," as the latter would only reinforce our anger. Genuine, positive prayer builds new links, and the anger will (hopefully) lessen over time.

Another helpful technique if you can't seem to forgive someone with whom you're upset is to simply imagine yourself forgiving them. What would that look like? What would you say? Imagine that scenario. Imagine it again. This simple practice can be effective in a fake-it-till-you-make it kind of way. By visualizing the act of forgiveness in your mind, you create the brain pathways that slowly transform imagined forgiveness into true forgiveness.

Culture Shock

Another important aspect to understand about neural links is that they often help us navigate the society in which we live. They are the explanation behind our automated sociocultural cues and responses, like handshakes. Someone says hello to us, and our brain knows that we're supposed to say hello in return. A person extends their hand toward us, and we know that we're supposed to shake it. In some churches, a person says to someone, "The Lord be with you," and the other person knows to respond, "And also with you." We could shout, "The Lord be with you!" in a crowded grocery store and probably hear someone in another aisle return, "And also with you!"

However, most of us are unconscious of our cultural expectations of others, so when things don't go according to what our brain expects, we feel uncomfortable, as if someone's gone off script. Unexpected events derail our brain from its regular, well-traveled neuronal roads and into uncharted territory. Of course that's uncomfortable. It's the biological basis behind culture shock.

I once hosted someone from another culture, and when I spoke to him, he would shake his head back and forth in reply. *Is he truly saying no to everything I say?* I wondered. *How rude!* But, after a little more communication, I learned that people in his culture shake their heads back and forth to indicate that they heard and understood what a person has said. He wasn't saying no after all; it was a simple cultural difference.

Chances are we've all experienced some degree of culture shock at one time or another. I'll share a personal experience that led to a cultural mistake I once made when I was young.

A Catholic family invited me to their church, and it was my first time attending a Catholic service. When the time came for communion, the family asked if I had been baptized. I replied that yes, I had been baptized. They meant, "Have you been baptized as a Catholic?" In which case, my answer would have been no; I was baptized in a Protestant church. But because I thought they asked if I had been baptized in general, I said yes, so they told me I could participate in communion.

I saw everyone line up, and I joined the queue. When it was my turn, the priest held out the communion wafer, and like a good Protestant, I picked up the bread from his hand and popped it in my mouth.

Aghast, the priest stared at me. He halted the service, pointed at me, and said, "This young man has chosen to take the power away from the priesthood and invest it in himself. He has desecrated this sacred ritual." I was escorted out of the church and felt terribly embarrassed.

First, I should have skipped this communion altogether. It was a Catholic communion, and I wasn't a Catholic, but I was culturally ignorant of the distinction between practices. Second, I should have watched the people in front of me take communion so that I could copy whatever they did once it was my turn. Other parishioners had let the priest place the wafer in their mouth. But I plucked the wafer from his hand—the way my church's culture did communion. In my friend's church's culture, this choice of mine carried a decidedly negative connotation.

Whenever we are immersed in a new culture, whether traveling to a foreign mission field or attending a church starkly different from our own, we're bound to make mistakes because our brain simply doesn't know what to do. And those mistakes tend to magnify our discomfort. To overcome this, we must first realize that culture shock is brain shock. Some of those well-traveled roads in our brain are no longer useful in new environments, so our brain must reorganize itself—even though it doesn't want to. That's the shock piece.

> Culture shock is brain shock.

By understanding that discomfort is normal and to be expected, we can sit in the discomfort and wait for our brain to rewire itself instead of running away from the mission field and whatever negative, uncomfortable feelings it may bring. The rewiring can sometimes take a while, but there is calm after the storm. Later, when we return to our culture, our brain has to rewire itself again, and reverse culture shock can set in. But again, it's a normal, biological process.

Culture shock isn't limited to foreign travel. Anyone making a lifestyle change can experience culture shock. Becoming sober, for example, goes beyond kicking an addiction. It's also leaving one culture and entering another. Cultures of addiction reinforce the behaviors of people with addictions, encouraging drug use and reinforcing denial. Simultaneously, addiction culture provides emotional support and a sense of belonging to active users. It's easy to understand why it can be such a challenge for addicts to leave this culture.

To help new clients at the rehab center understand the importance of culture, I conducted an unusual Bible study. I would host it in the pig barn on the property, and we'd sit on overturned buckets among the sows. It didn't really matter what subject we studied; what mattered was that everyone smelled themselves when we were done. We all stunk like pigs and manure, but our collective stench made my point.

When the addicts did something good for themselves, like attend Bible study or make a small positive change, but chose to remain within their drug's culture, I explained that they would continue to witness addictive behaviors, continue to expose themselves to harmful triggers, and continue to make themselves vulnerable to peer pressure from fellow users to "act normal" and return to using. Just like staying inside the smelly pig barn would make them smell, staying within their drug culture would reinforce all their brain's links to their old life. So yes, study the Bible, I'd tell them, but also get out of the pig barn entirely.

Of course, sober culture can be intimidating, confusing, and lonely to anyone not versed in it. An addict might have enjoyed a kind of social status in their drug's culture, but in sober culture they have none. In fact, a common complaint among clients was that they didn't know how to be social without their substance of choice. Whenever we planned recreational trips, many clients would volunteer to stay home and work to avoid the stress and pressure of trying to socialize while sober. They didn't know how to have fun without their drug of choice and felt awkward. To overcome that, we'd talk about how to make a friend without sharing a drink or a smoke and what topics to talk about when meeting new people.

This same lesson of changing one's culture applies to anyone working to make a life change. We have to get out of our own pig barns and into environments that will support our hard work toward transformation.

It's common to experience culture shock when beginning or renewing a faith journey, addict or not. Many of my clients expressed specific frustration with the culture shock of church. They didn't have a clue as to what was going on during services. The pastors and parishioners seemed to speak a different language, and they didn't know how or when to participate. That's why I developed a comprehensive religious education program as part of a client's rehabilitation. I wanted to enculturate them to the church environment, ensuring that they were as or more educated than the average parishioner when it came to the Bible, theology, church history, and denominations. That way, when they entered a church, they knew what to anticipate, they understood the language, and they felt comfortable participating and growing in their faith.

We must prepare for culture shock in whatever lifestyle change we make. Whether we're moving out of a culture of anger and into a culture of peace, or a culture of poor eating habits to one of healthy habits, culture shock will probably happen. If you attend a church for the first time, expect culture shock and be willing to work with it. Don't let the temporary discomfort discourage you from further attendance.

> We must prepare for culture shock in whatever lifestyle change we make.

We want to embark on our journey of change while remaining fully aware that we'll need to learn new coping mechanisms, establish support systems, identify personal values, and develop a new identity. This also means that we must work on integrating into a new culture and have patience and grace for ourselves, knowing there will be discomfort, awkwardness, miscommunication, and mistakes.

Achieving Positive Impact

I was once teaching material on neural linking to a pastoral leadership class, and one of the members told me how he used this very concept to create a memorable sermon. He was giving a talk on 2 Corinthians 2:15, which mentions a "pleasing aroma of Christ" (NIV). He arranged for people to place freshly cooked bacon near the air vents during the sermon. As he spoke of a pleasing smell, the odor of bacon began to permeate the sanctuary. The pastor related to me that this sermon is the most remembered and cited among his parishioners to this day. He used the power of neural linking to achieve a lasting impact with his church's community.

(As a side note, smells can link powerfully with memory and emotion. Smell sensations transmit directly to the emotional and memory centers of the brain, while the other senses must go to a switchboard in the brain first. This is why certain smells bring up memories so easily.[28])

Before working as a chaplain for the rehabilitation center, I first completed an internship there as an evening manager. I was responsible for making sure residents got along and followed the rules while the daytime staff were off duty, and I administered random drug tests to ensure program compliance. On my first day on the job, I went around the dormitories to introduce myself.

I said hello to the first resident I saw, to which he replied, "Who the (bleep) are you?" before taking a drunk, clumsy swing at me. He had snuck alcohol into the facility. Needless to say, I did not return home with warm, fuzzy feelings of having made a positive difference in the lives of others. I mostly wondered what I had gotten myself into.

In another story, a friend of mine, moved by compassion, once let a homeless man stay the night on his couch. The next morning, my friend woke up to find the man was already gone, as well as quite a few of my friend's possessions. "This is the last time I help these people," he lamented to me. This friend had also been mentoring disadvantaged youth, but unfortunately, this negative experience with the homeless man had left such a bad taste in my friend's mouth that he resigned altogether from his position as a mentor.

Some people tend to romanticize the poor and marginalized, pitying them as innocents beaten down by life. They also tend to expect people in need to show immense gratitude when receiving help. Schools and churches, for example, often send kids or parishioners to homeless shelters to volunteer. Those schools and churches assume their volunteers will feel proud of their service and that their experience will foster compassion for the people they served, which is often the case. However, the people served may not always react or behave well or express gratitude at all.

My point in sharing these cautionary tales is not to discourage others from helping people who are struggling but to understand that positive emotions aren't guaranteed to flow after we perform acts of mercy, and not all experiences of helping others will be positive.[29] The poor and marginalized show the same range of emotions and dysfunctions as everyone else.

Nevertheless, a discouraging service experience doesn't have to be the reason why a person steers clear of helping others in the future. That's why we do not want to leave our emotions to chance as they relate to helping others. We can intentionally develop hearts of service by reframing negative events as valuable learning experiences, thereby linking positive feelings with service to others. This link can be established with an added educational element.

> We can intentionally develop hearts of service by reframing negative events as valuable learning experiences.

To help people have positive experiences with serving others, schools, churches, and organizations must educate volunteers before and after service events. Not only does this twofold approach help everyone set realistic expectations ahead of their service, but a proper debriefing after service work also helps people process any negative emotions they might have experienced within the proper context, turning a person's bad experience into an opportunity for growth.

Imagine a friendly, outgoing volunteer serving food at a shelter. The volunteer asks a resident how their day is going, and the resident completely ignores the volunteer. The volunteer might feel insulted or hurt. After the event, the volunteer's service leader can help the volunteer process their disheartening experience. Together, they may consider reasons why the resident responded poorly. Perhaps the person being served was experiencing withdrawal, or the volunteer reminded them of someone who hurt them in the past, or maybe life has beaten them up to the extent that they didn't know how to positively respond to the volunteer's kindness on that particular day.

Teaching mercy in the face of negativity can be an impetus to cultivate even greater compassion in the future. When I struggle in my service to others, I remind myself that if I limit my charity to people who show gratitude in some meaningful way, then I am neglecting the people who need it most. And to be honest, those who lash out at the very hands trying to help them probably *do* need the most help.

The Power of Personal Testimonies

Another way to use brain knots to our advantage is to make good ones, healthy ones. And we can do that by sharing our testimonies. It's no mystery as to why Revelation 12:11 says the devil is overcome by people's testimonies. When others share the ways in which God has provided for them, we're able to draw parallels to our own lives. Their hope becomes our hope. Their testimonies and breakthroughs can carry us through our own rough spots when God seems distant or uncaring or when we're waiting on him, feeling convinced that he's just procrastinating. By sharing with others how God has come through for us in challenging times, we link together the ideas of challenges and God's support, and this neural link begets more faith and hope.

> When others share the ways in which God has provided for them, we're able to draw parallels to our own lives. Their hope becomes our hope.

Similar to the power of personal testimonies is the power of memorials. At times throughout the Bible, God commanded people to create memorials to remember certain meaningful events. In Genesis 28:10–22, for example, Jacob erected a pillar in Bethel to commemorate a powerful vision God had given him. This pillar served as both a physical and visual reminder of God's promise to him, helping Jacob increase his faith and the faith of everyone who laid eyes on the memorial.

In Joshua 4:1–8, God parted the Jordan River for the Israelites, who took twelve stones from the riverbed and placed them on the riverbank. The stones memorialized God's miraculous intervention and reminded future generations of his power and goodness.

First Samuel 7:7–12 relates how God gave Israel a miraculous victory over their neighboring enemies, the Philistines. In remembrance of God's intervention, Samuel placed a large stone between the warring towns to declare God's faithfulness to all who saw the stone monument.

We, too, can create memorials of our own. One simple memorial is to write a list of our prayers, leaving space to record how and when God answers them. All too often, our answered prayers go unnoticed because we forgot we prayed them in the first place. This kind of list can uplift us whenever we're feeling discouraged, lost, or hopeless.

We all need reminders of God's mercy and kindness, and memorials accomplish precisely that. They link together a memory and a symbolic representation of God's faithfulness, prompting us to recall the times when God has come through for us. And if we revisit these times whenever we're faced with a new challenge, then we carry with us into the present the trust and confidence we experienced in the past, increasing our faith and decreasing feelings of anxiety.

Counseling

If we experience or have experienced trauma, the event and the negative emotions associated with it become linked in our brain. Then, whenever we remember the event or talk about it with another person, we often trigger the negative emotions all over again because of this neural link. And as many of us know, the pain of reliving traumatic experiences and emotions can be debilitating and discouraging, leading us to believe we might never heal from them.

Counseling provides a safe, caring atmosphere for retelling stories of trauma. The act of retelling painful experiences to a compassionate counselor helps a person relink their experiences with feelings of safety, which helps the pain lose some of its sting.

> Counseling provides a safe, caring atmosphere for retelling stories of trauma.

For example, a soldier relating a painful war experience will likely reexperience the pain while retelling their story because their painful experience is linked with painful emotions. But if the soldier shares their story with a counselor, a support group, or with caring friends, the soldier will gradually replace their painful emotions with feelings of safety found within those relationships.

As many people who have shared their stories of trauma can attest, the first telling can be incredibly difficult, unpleasant, and uncomfortable, but after several retellings, it gets easier. And lots of people will need to repeat the same story over and over again, and it's easy to think, *This story again? Time to move on, Mr. Stuck Pants*. But the reality is that a person may need to retell a story several times before they're able to successfully relink positive thoughts and emotions to their experience. And with each retelling, they actively engage in the therapeutic process, casting off pain and strengthening new, healthy neural connections.

Summary

Neurons that fire together wire together, creating links and knots in our brain whenever we think, feel, experience, or act on things in tandem. If you have a couple of scary run-ins with spiders, you might wire fear with bugs. Or if a parent has a fear of bugs, you might wire fear with bugs, too, since you regularly witness an influential person in your life experience fear in association with bugs.

You can apply this same wiring mechanism to serious social issues, like race. If someone has a negative experience with a person of a different race or listens to negative narratives or stereotypes about people of that race, then they risk linking a person's skin color with prejudicial beliefs and perpetuating racism. And while our society has a long way to go in combating racism, you can combat harmful beliefs in your own thought life by seeking out narratives and experiences that challenge the negative ones. Pursue relationships with people who offer new and different perspectives that enable you to rewire or forge new brain links.

To develop neural links that work positively for you, first take note of any and all potential triggers that set off unhealthy behavioral patterns in you. Does a certain person trigger your anger? Are you programmed to binge on sugar or buy a pack of cigarettes when under stress? Then you must destroy the destructive links by forging new ones, and forging new links often requires training new emotions.

Emotional training involves practicing positive thoughts, utilizing a support system of people who encourage you, and putting yourself in situations that evoke specific feelings so that you can train your responses into habits. You can also train your emotions by practicing emotional reframing. You might not be able to control your initial feelings, but you can control how you process and react to them and, therefore, change them. Putting yourself in someone else's shoes as a means of practicing emotional reframing is particularly helpful. It invites curiosity instead of judgment or blame, and it allows you to explore the reasons behind a person's choices and behavior, all of which help us to be more merciful and forgiving.

Making any life change will involve culture shock. Culture shock is brain shock, and you're bound to make mistakes and missteps whenever you're outside your "normal." It's uncomfortable, yes, but you can prepare for it by establishing support systems, practicing new coping mechanisms, and remaining patient with yourself.

You can utilize the power of neural linking to achieve great, positive impact on your culture and the world around you. Doing community service with supportive friends, for example, can link positive emotions and memories with acts of service. Add to this service work an orientation and debriefing to regulate expectations and put negative experiences into proper context, and you just might produce a service-oriented life and find true joy in it.

Don't be afraid to seek counseling in times of personal change. A counselor can help you unlink pain and negative thoughts surrounding traumatic experiences and relink healthy thoughts and emotions instead. This therapeutic process takes time, but throughout the process you strengthen new, healthy neural links.

Reflect

1.   Imagine you are a robot. What programs run automatically as part of your software? What initiates the running of those programs?

2.   Write the word *God* in the center of a piece of paper. Then draw lines extending out from the word *God,* and at the end of each line, write a concept that you connect with the idea of God, such as loving, authoritarian, mean, sovereign, or distant. This isn't a test on what the Bible says about God but how you feel about him, so be honest with yourself.

     Then draw new lines extending out from each new concept and connect it to other concepts to which they may be linked in your brain. Maybe you link God with love, in which case you would draw lines connecting the concept of love to a memorable, loving experience you have had or a personal belief about love. Ultimately, this picture represents your web of neural links. What concepts would you like to change, remove, or add?

What concepts are missing? What characteristics from your own parents or caregivers connect to your idea of God? For example, if your dad was emotionally distant, do you view God as emotionally distant? Or if you had to earn the approval of your parents or caregivers, do you also feel that you need to earn God's love?

3. Identify an area in which you are struggling with change. How might culture shock play a role in your struggle or complicate your adjusting to your new way of life?

4. How can you help others overcome culture shock when attending your church, particularly new believers and unbelievers?

5. Identify at least one person whom you are struggling to forgive. What small steps can you take to move forward in the forgiveness process? How can you reframe your emotions as they relate to this person?

6. Recall a time when God did something wonderful in your life. What type of memorial could you create to remind yourself of his faithfulness?

Chapter 4

The Power of the Imagination: It Becomes Reality

Try this little exercise. Imagine yourself sitting inside a dark movie theater, having just watched the closing credits. You stand up and shuffle toward the exit. You push open the exit door, emerge from the dark theater, and step into the bright, noonday sun. Ouch! Burning eyeballs! Guess what? Your body likely reacted to this exercise by constricting your pupils as if you had *actually* stepped into the bright light.

Scientists Bruno Laeng and Unni Sulutvedt performed this same exercise with research participants in a lab. Their findings showed that people's pupils do, in fact, dilate or constrict in response to imagined darkness or bright light.[30] This is because the same parts of the brain that fire in real circumstances also fire in imaginary ones. What we can learn from their findings is that our imagination plays a critical role when it comes to forming and changing neural pathways, linking neurons, and establishing automatic behaviors.

Physiologist Lokman Wong's brain research upholds Laeng and Sulutvedt's and further shows that performing an action, perceiving an action, and imagining an action all rely on the same brain paths.[31] In other words, the brain can't tell the difference.[32] This means that imagining an action is nearly the same as actually doing it. It activates similar neurons as if you were doing the action yourself, thereby facilitating a learning process that allows you to learn by observing others.[33]

When we learned to tie our shoes, for example, we probably observed someone else do it and then practiced doing it ourselves by replicating their motions. The reverse is also true: other people learn and shape their brains by observing us, which serves as a good reminder that we are sometimes role models whether or not we intend to be.

Imagining an action is nearly the same as actually doing it.

Neuroscientist Vittorio Gallese states, "To perceive an action is equivalent to internally simulating it,"[34] and I would add that this internal simulation also influences the shaping of our character. If I imagine myself punching a coworker in the face, I don't risk job loss and jail time like I would if I actually punched them. But if I frequently imagine punching them, then I risk altering my character at a neuronal level because I would have normalized aggressive, violent behavior. We can use this same concept to tell the difference between a temptation and a "thought sin."[35]

A sinful thought is a temptation, and we choose what we do with that sinful thought, whereas a sin is a decision to hold on to the sinful thought, allowing our brain to steer us in the direction of the temptation. Ultimately, the point is that whatever we think about, whatever we consume with our senses, and whatever kind of company we keep are critical. It all influences who we are at a brain level and can help or hinder our moral goals. In light of these research findings, Philippians 4:8 takes on a deeper meaning: "Whatever is true, whatever is noble, whatever is right, whatever is pure, whatever is lovely, whatever is admirable—if anything is excellent or praiseworthy—think about such things" (NIV).

> A sinful thought is a temptation, and we choose what we do with that sinful thought, whereas a sin is a decision to hold on to the sinful thought, allowing our brain to steer us in the direction of the temptation.

Numerous fascinating research studies reveal the power of imagination and bodily action, and these studies arrive at the same conclusion: practicing an action in your imagination can improve performance just like practicing it for real. Take the research of renowned neurophysiologist Alvaro Pascual-Leone, who designed an experiment around piano practice. Participants in the study were randomly assigned to a group that physically practiced the piano, a group that mentally practiced piano, or a control group that did not practice in any way. The first two groups that either physically or mentally practiced piano did so for two hours a day over a five-day span of time.

The results of Pascual-Leone's experiment showed that both the physical and mental practice groups demonstrated improved performance. "Mental practice alone seems to be sufficient to promote the modulation of neural circuits involved in the early stages of motor skill learning," Pascual-Leone states. "This modulation not only results in a marked performance improvement but also seems to place the subjects at an advantage for further skill learning with minimal physical practice."[36] In other words, practicing a skill in our mind improves our physical performance of that skill and helps us better develop it over time.

Neuroscientists Guang Yue and Kelly Cole conducted a similar experiment but around physical exercise. Their findings illustrated the same impact of imagination in physical performance and in a dramatic way. You might be thinking, *Wait a minute! I can sit on my couch and imagine my way to a ripped beach body?* Well, in a way.

Yue and Cole assigned participants to one of three groups: one group physically performed muscle contractions, another group imagined contracting their muscles, and the control group did not exercise at all. The first two groups either exercised physically or in their imaginations for four weeks, five sessions per week. The physical exercise group improved their muscle strength by 30 percent, and the imagination group improved by 22 percent.[37] Unsurprisingly, the control group showed no change, but at least the participants in that group walked away with the positive feeling of having gained advanced scientific knowledge.

While the participants who imagined exercising did not improve muscle strength as much as the group that physically exercised, an increase still happened. So we might not be able to imagine our way to a fully fit beach body, but our imagination can effect change. And if we combine imaginary exercise with physical exercise, we can boost our improvement even more.

Because our imagination impacts who we are, we must ask ourselves if we are thinking of ways to do good, to help others, and to successfully resist temptation, or are we imagining giving up on whatever change we want to make? Are we imagining worst-case scenarios and constructing highways in our brain for anxiety, or are we imagining the best and fostering hope? Do we imagine revenge or forgiveness? It reminds me of a client who said, "When it came to cheating on my wife, it happened so easily because I had already done it a thousand times in my mind." We must remember that we create automatic behaviors and habits in our imagination as easily as we do through behavioral actions.

> We create automatic behaviors and habits in our imagination as easily as we do through behavioral actions.

Practice Makes Automatic, Not Perfect

We know now that we can create automatic behaviors using our imagination, but what happens if we practice incorrectly? In a study on springboard divers, cognitive neuroscientist Catherine Reed conducted experiments on the speed of the imagination. Novices and experts were quickly able to mentally picture a dive, but divers of intermediate skill were slower. As stated by Reed, "Intermediates may be relatively slowed by greater amounts of non-automatized knowledge, as compared with the automatized knowledge of experts or the sparse knowledge of novices."[38]

Novices could imagine performing the dive in any haphazard fashion since they didn't know any better. Of course, if they were to translate this imagined performance into an actual one, they would likely see poor results. Intermediates, on the other hand, know the proper mechanics of performing a dive but must consciously think about their training in order to imagine doing it accurately and effectively. The expert diver who has performed the dive repeatedly has automatized the mechanics of a dive on a subconscious level and thus performs both real and imaginary dives rapidly and accurately.

A self-defense trainer who often worked with law enforcement once told me a story about the consequences of practicing incorrectly. The trainer would share techniques on how to disarm a suspect with a gun, and the officers would practice with each other. One officer would play the bad guy with a fake weapon, and the other officer would practice disarming him. The officer would then hand the gun back to the other officer and repeat the drill. Their repeated performance of this drill would automatize their disarming technique, right? Unfortunately, in a later, real-life situation, the officer disarmed a suspect but then promptly handed the gun back to the suspect! Practice doesn't make perfect; it makes automatic. Because handing the gun back was part of the drill, it, too, became automatic. Needless to say, the officers had to develop a new way of practicing the disarming technique.

Practice doesn't make perfect; it makes automatic.

These studies reveal that we must imagine correctly if we want to perform correctly, and that requires our brain to draw upon experience. If we are a newbie at learning a skill, be it physical, mental, social, or emotional, we have to take time to learn and practice that skill. And once we've gained enough experience, we can slowly think through how we're performing it to gradually ingrain that skill into who we are. In the words of my son's kindergarten teacher, "Practice makes permanent."

The Power of Perception

In the last chapter we talked about how our brains, chock-full of their own highways and links, impact how we see the world and what we observe. And once we master a skill or behavior, we start to observe entirely new and different things. It changes our perception. The next couple of studies we're going to examine are similar to those we read in the previous section, but they also highlight the importance of perception.

Behavioral neurologist Salvatore Aglioti conducted an experiment on the ability to predict the accuracy of a basketball player's free throws. The participants included professional players, expert fans who watched countless basketball games, and players who were new to the game. Aglioti found that experienced, professional basketball players predict the outcome of free shots earlier and more accurately than those who have no direct experience playing the game.[39]

Whereas the expert game watchers and novices relied on the trajectory of the ball to make their predictions, players with physical basketball experience were able to better predict the fate of the ball based on the thrower's body cues. This reveals the importance of bodily experience in perception. As stated by Aglioti, "Elite athletes, but not novices and expert watchers, can 'read' the kinematics of the observed action."[40] In short, basketball players with physical expertise possess superior perceptual ability over and above people with mere visual experience, who were unable to register the significance and implications of body movement. Only the experienced were able to "see." A general principle to infer from this study is that seeing without doing is not enough to achieve excellence.

> Seeing without doing is not enough to achieve
> excellence.

Aglioti supplemented his initial experiment with brain scans of professional basketball players while they watched other athletes shoot baskets and kick soccer balls. In their brain scans, he observed increased motor excitability when they watched basketball shots and no increase in activity in relation to soccer kicks. This experiment confirmed an earlier study on professional dancers.

Cognitive neuroscientist Beatriz Calvo-Merino scanned the brains of ballet dancers, capoeira dancers (described as a dance style with moves similar to ballet), and non-dancers when observing various dance movements. The subjects' brain activity increased in relation to moves that they themselves perform but not to moves that were merely similar. Calvo-Merino determined that a person's action observation system is precisely attuned to his or her individual bodily experience. To generalize, what people see or what captures their attention depends upon what they know.[41]

These experiments highlight the importance of experience as it relates to our perception. Our worldview and what we register both intuitively and subconsciously is linked to what we are familiar with and the actions we are accustomed to performing. Mere "head knowledge" is not enough to train our perception. It requires actual performance.

Let's briefly summarize what we've learned from studies on the imagination. First, what we imagine becomes who we are, and it impacts what we are capable of doing in the future, good or bad. Further, we must pair what we practice in our imagination with physical practice so that we train correctly. And with this training, we change how we see the world and how we see ourselves. That's how we can influence our spiritual development and formation for the better. When we imagine living righteously and put it into practice, we improve our walk with God. We're better able to grow in wisdom so that we "see" new things, new solutions, and new opportunities to serve.

Imagination and Moral Development

As we learned from Aglioti's basketball study, we gain some degree of proficiency through observational learning, and the same holds true when it comes to our moral development. We can observe the virtuous activities of our personal role models and listen to sermons about doing good, and those can help us achieve a novice level of virtuous performance.

But much like the basketball fans who fared poorly in predicting free throws, we can't strictly rely on observations of virtuous people. This approach proves insufficient when it comes to gaining wisdom, practicing righteous living, and developing an orientation toward sacrificial service. We have to go beyond passive observation of church services and conceptual discussions of ethics and put our virtues into practice. We have to take action and get involved in tangible activities if we want to change our worldview. Let's discuss activities and exercises that rely on the imagination and support moral development.

> We have to go beyond passive observation of church services and conceptual discussions of ethics and put our virtues into practice.

Development through Roleplay

Since we can shape our brains as easily in the imagination as through actual performance, we can use imaginative roleplay to enhance moral education. Think about it: Should we merely tell kids (and parishioners) what is right, or should we give them opportunities to practice doing right? When we actively engage in imaginary scenarios, we're better prepared for tricky, uncomfortable situations we're likely to experience in the future. However, that's not to say that roleplay and verbal teaching are mutually exclusive approaches to moral education. In fact, discussions around ethical thought problems can augment moral education.

One fictional ethical dilemma, popular in ethics textbooks, is called "the trolley problem." It's an imaginary exercise that underlines moral decision-making. Many versions of this dilemma exist, but the basic structure requires you to imagine yourself as a passenger on a trolley (or train) hurtling toward several people tied to the tracks. But you also have the power to switch the trolley to another track on which only one person is tied, killing one instead of several. A person who holds a utilitarian ethical view would change tracks so that only one person dies, but other perspectives insist that one should not participate in killing and leave the trolley on its course.

While this trolley problem is useful in teaching differences among ethical systems, it's far from realistic. It's much more effective to present moral dilemmas and facilitate roleplay exercises that people are likely to encounter in their personal lives.

Nancy Sherman, Georgetown ethicist, relates how role models leading roleplays can effectively engage the imagination in ethical instruction. Sherman provides an example from her time as the ethics chair at the United States Naval Academy. As part of a lesson on courage, a naval airman led the class in a simulation of a mission he himself had experienced during which fellow pilots were lost. Following the lesson, a debriefing took place regarding emotion, grief, and retaining your humanity in the face of loss during combat. Sherman states, "We tend to focus on the abstract and forget the riveting power of an enactment to immerse a class in a gripping and nuanced discussion of a moral topic."[42]

Imaginative roleplay can also help us overcome sin by training and automatizing proper reactions to temptation. We can devise and rehearse specific plans in our minds, such as "I will do X in the event of Y." That way, when such an event occurs, we'll respond appropriately and instinctively.

An example of the efficacy of imaginary roleplay comes from a former client named Shawn. Shawn was an alcoholic and drug addict, and he feared how he would handle his first weekend pass to visit his family in Denver.

"Will I be able to resist temptations," he worried, "or will I be one of those guys who disappears on a pass and never comes back?"

"Imagine running into your ex-girlfriend," I started. "Maybe she calls you up and invites you to a party where there will be alcohol. Maybe she shows up at your door, drugs in tow. Imagine yourself refusing and turning her away. Imagine running the other direction and imagine this multiple times."

While nothing harmful happened on Shawn's first weekend pass, he did share an interesting story with us a few passes later.

"I was walking downtown when I heard a voice yell, 'Shawn! Shawn!' I look over and actually see my ex-girlfriend! She was sitting by herself at a street-facing patio bar. She called me over to join her, but the next thing I knew, my feet had turned around, and I was walking away. It wasn't even a conscious decision. I didn't have time to answer her calls before I was a block away, and I kept walking!"

Shawn's imaginary roleplay successfully prepared him to resist a tempting situation. He had programmed his brain to respond in a positive, healthy way that helped him protect his sobriety.

In a similar example from the rehab facility, we used an imaginary exercise that I termed "Where does that road lead?" In this exercise, we asked clients to imagine themselves having to face a realistic decision. Then we had them imagine their reaction to the decision to its full completion—consequences and all.

One client's answer to this exercise stands out in my mind. He had reached four years of sobriety, and I asked him, "How have you stayed away from meth for so long? It is such a powerful drug that so few overcome."

"I have a wife and a young daughter now," he answered. "Whenever I think of seeing old drug friends or using a drug, I remember, 'Where does that road lead?' And then I imagine myself losing my wife and daughter, being homeless again, and recalling my friend Chuck dying from an overdose in a gas station bathroom. The desire loses its appeal after that."

Instead of focusing on using and the immediate high, the client shifted his focus and imagined the long-term consequences, and it forestalled destructive behavior.

Development through Story

Stories are also essential to moral formation. According to religious studies professor Charlene Burns, stories can be more formational than discursive reasoning because they engage the imagination.[43] Scientific journalist Jeremy Tsu echoes Burns and explains that stories function as a training simulator, a safe arena within which to rehearse the skills necessary for a successful social life. People use narratives to communicate with each other and to teach children which behaviors are virtuous and which ones are not. Narratives themselves are role models.[44]

We enter narratives by way of the imagination, and our neurons fire as if we are in the stories themselves.[45] As stated by moral philosopher Alistair MacIntyre, "I can only answer the question 'What am I to do?' if I can answer the prior question 'Of what story or stories do I find myself a part?'"[46] And if we find ourselves part of negative stories, then we need to find and identify with new ones.

> We enter narratives by way of the imagination, and our neurons fire as if we are in the stories themselves.

A client who was a recovering alcoholic once told us that his favorite story was the nursery rhyme *Little Boy Blue*:

> Little boy blue, come blow your horn,
> The sheep's in the meadow, the cows in the corn,
> But where is the boy who looks after the sheep?
> He is under the haystack, fast asleep.
> Will you wake him? No, not I,
> For if I do, he's sure to cry.

It turned out that this client came from a family of cowboys, and he did not enjoy living on the farm in the same ways that his brothers did. As a result, he was often teased and abused. Whenever his brothers would look for him, he would hide in the haystacks. This client saw himself as *Little Boy Blue*, sleeping, hiding, and crying in the haystack. That was the story he internalized about himself. Recovery for him meant finding a new story, the Christian one, and anchoring his identity in it.

Again, to see, to imagine, and to do utilize similar neural pathways, and we can harness the power of story to benefit moral education. Countless resources are readily available, ranging from Scripture to the lives of exemplary Christians, parables, liturgical practices, music, and church history. Those serving in ministry will want to consider learning to become good storytellers so that they can blend impactful narratives into their preaching. That's not to say that stories are a replacement for solid biblical interpretation, but they help biblical interpretations stick with listeners.

Stories can also help us reach people for Jesus. Reporter Al Hsu described in *Christianity Today* how Christian gospel presentations are often "like spoilers that tell you what happened but take all the suspense and delight out of the journey."[47] Put another way, we short circuit narrative imagination and jump to the conclusion: God loves you, Jesus died for you, now pray this prayer. Of course this is critical information, but how we relay that information is also important, not just that we say it. As Hsu states, "We can recover the imagination, a sense of wonder at a world of mystery and discovery. We can invite people to join us on a long-term experiential journey that's full of twists and turns but nevertheless infused with hope."[48]

Development through Bible Study

The use of imagination offers a unique approach to Bible study too. This approach differs greatly from discussing the meaning of passages, the original Greek or Hebrew text, the historical context, or the practical life applications. The imaginative approach to Bible study inserts us into the stories themselves, engaging both our emotions and our intellect.

> The imaginative approach to Bible study inserts us into the stories themselves, engaging both our emotions and our intellect.

In his book *Spiritual Exercises*, Ignatius of Loyola, a Spanish priest and theologian from the 1500s, instructs readers to imagine witnessing and participating in various events throughout Jesus' life. Originally meant to be done in silence and solitude for a month, this exercise is designed to improve one's discernment and to become an ally with God and his purposes through contemplation, action, prayer, service, emotion, and reason. Ignatius of Loyola's method for this imaginative exercise is as follows.

1. Pick an action-packed passage from the Gospels.

2. Read the passage multiple times, perhaps six or seven, to fully comprehend the details and the setting. Pause between each reading to let what you've read sink in.

Then imagine the scene using your senses. For example, if you insert yourself into the story of Jesus calming the storm, then imagine the smell of saltwater. How does it feel when the boat rocks? Imagine the grunts and groans coming from the disciples struggling to sail the boat or the soft sounds of Jesus sleeping undisturbed.

3. Now imagine yourself as one of the characters in the scene and let it play out. Imagine your interactions and conversations with the other characters. Let yourself feel and take notice of those feelings.

    To hearken back to the storm-calming passage again, imagine yourself as one of the disciples struggling with the boat—your muscles straining and your frustration building—until everything suddenly goes calm. Then revisit the story as a different character. Picture yourself as Jesus, full of confidence. Lose yourself in the story and let it affect you. Don't worry about practical applications.

4. Reflect afterward. What did you experience during this imaginary exercise? What moments stood out? How did you feel? What might you need to consider from this exercise as you go about your day or as you lie down to rest?[49]

The steps from Ignatius of Loyola's exercise above bring Bible stories to life. And we can soak up both the lessons and values from those stories and embed them into our very character in new, profound ways.

Development through Prayer

Imagination also invigorates prayer. When I began to pray with my wife, I realized there was a significant gulf between us in how we prayed. For example, I prayed, "Lord, help heal my friend's knee as he goes into surgery today." Bam. Done. My wife, however, prayed for this friend at length. At first, I didn't know how she did it. It's a knee…do I pray for each bone?

No, my wife prayed as if she were the person awaiting surgery. She prayed for his anxiety, prayed that the people around him would be a source of encouragement, for the nurses and doctors, that the medicine would have no side effects, for a speedy recovery, and that the pain would be negligible. She put herself in his shoes. I had an awakening that day in my own prayer life. If I imagine myself as the person for whom I am praying or imagine myself in their situation, I'm able to incorporate many more thoughtful details into my prayers.

Imaginative prayer fosters empathy too. Imagine yourself as your enemy and consider their hurts and concerns. What might have led them to do whatever it is that caused or causes you pain? Your enemy might need love, help with anxiety or depression, mercy, understanding, accountability, or someone to stop their spiral of self-destructive thoughts and behaviors. In imagining these details, you might find yourself feeling compassion instead of anger, which wires new connections in your brain.

Praying for the needs of our enemies in our imagination does not mean we are excusing their behavior. Sin is sin regardless of where it comes from. We don't have to pray that they win the lottery, but we can pray for what's best for them. We can pray for their spiritual life and their relationships with God and others. Sometimes we might even pray for justice.

I once asked a client of mine to write about the difference between God's mercy and his justice. His answer was powerful. He told me that God's justice *was* God's mercy. If the police hadn't caught him selling drugs and he hadn't spent time in jail, he would have never changed, never gotten to know God, and would have likely died on the streets. God issued him justice, which was also mercy.

Using the imagination in prayer can also assist in the healing of traumatic memories. In his discussion on the spiritual exercises of Ignatius of Loyola, a monk named Joseph recorded the following situation in his own life.[50] The monk had received feedback from others who said he seemed to carry bitterness, and they believed his bitterness was manifesting itself as harshness. The monk chose to bring this concern to God in prayer, asking God to help him remember situations from his past that might be contributing to his bitterness.

> Using the imagination in prayer can also assist in the healing of traumatic memories.

Among other memories, the monk remembered a time when two boys in high school bullied him. Instead of reliving the scene, he visualized an entirely new one. First, he imagined himself forgiving the two boys. Next, he imagined returning to the scene with Jesus by his side and witnessing the boys' confusion at the sight of Jesus. He pictured Jesus forgiving the boys and teaching them how to be loving. The monk then visualized himself talking to Jesus about the situation afterward and receiving Jesus' love and encouragement. Once the monk was able to imagine his teenage self smiling, he knew he had healed from the traumatic memory.

Like the monk, we can heal from painful, traumatic memories by recasting them toward healing. Below is a summary of the steps the monk took to heal from his traumatic memories through prayer.

1. Begin by thinking about God's presence, love, and desire to see you heal. This puts the rest of the exercise into proper context and primes the brain to create positive links and replace painful ones.

2. Ask the Holy Spirit to help you recall the traumatic memory in question or a painful memory you may have forgotten.

3. Give yourself space, time, and quietness to allow the memory to surface.

4. Walk back into these memories with Jesus and imagine what would happen with him beside you.

5. Thank Jesus for healing.[51]

Remember that prayer does not always need to be expressed in words. We can pray in images when we simply can't find the words to say. Personally, when I don't know how or what to pray for someone, or when a situation seems too big or complex, I turn to my imagination. I imagine the person or situation resting in my hands as I lift them up to Jesus.

We learned in the previous chapter that rewiring neural links takes time, so healing from traumatic memories may not come right away. It's very possible you'll need to revisit these steps more than once, and that's perfectly normal.

> Prayer does not always have to be expressed in words. We can pray in images when we simply can't find the words to say.

Summary

Imagination is a powerful force for shaping and changing your brain. Because the brain activates and reinforces the same pathways when imagining an action as it does when performing an action, you become what you imagine. That means your imagination can help or hinder your moral development.

> You become what you imagine.

When imagining yourself facing a temptation, for example, it's easy to think, *I wouldn't do that in real life though*. Not so fast. What you imagine changes you little by little, so what you assume is impossible in real life slowly becomes ever more possible. That's why it's important to imagine yourself doing the right thing so that you establish it as an automatic response. That is, you will do the right thing without having to think twice about it because you've trained yourself to respond that way. And one of the most effective ways to train those responses is through imaginary roleplays that allow you to rehearse your reactions to realistic scenarios.

Stories offer another impactful approach to moral education. They function as role models to children and adults alike, teaching right from wrong, what's important, and how to exist in society and the world in general. To take the power of story even further, you can picture yourself as part of a story, which is a unique approach to Bible study. In imagining all the rich details within a story, you deepen your understanding not only of the event but also of the people involved. It engages both your emotions and your intellect. This effective practice dates back centuries and is just as relevant and worthy of implementing today as it was back then.

In the same way, your imagination can boost your prayer life. When you imagine yourself in someone else's shoes, whether they're the shoes of a friend or foe, you gain perspective and become better able to pray thoroughly and thoughtfully. And if you imagine yourself as your enemy and consider their pain, hurt, and challenges, you foster both compassion and empathy. It's not always going to be easy, but pray for whatever is best for them. Pray for their spiritual walk, and remember that you aren't limited to praying with words. You can pray visually by painting pictures in your mind.

> If you imagine yourself as your enemy and consider their pain, hurt, and challenges, you foster both compassion and empathy.

Your imagination can help facilitate the healing of traumatic memories. When revisiting a painful conversation or event, walk back into that memory with Jesus by your side. Reconstruct what would happen if you had perceived Jesus as present in that moment, engaging and conversing with you about your feelings and reactions.

It is important to note that in discussing the power of imagination, you are not altering physical reality through the power of thought, as some religious or self-help groups might suggest.[52] Rather, you are using your imagination to strengthen and link neural pathways that relate to actually performing an action and to associated emotions, motivators, and perceptual ability. Your outer reality is then altered by way of new personal behaviors induced by imagination-altered neurochemistry.

While I draw conclusions about moral formation from recent scientific studies on neuroscience and imagination, the connections discovered among imagination, training in the faith, and character formation are not new. Nevertheless, neurological studies that support imaginative practices through empirical data emphasize the need for such practices. They have the potential to direct those who have neglected their imaginations to rediscover imaginative resources already present within their cultural or spiritual traditions.

Reflect

1. What area of your life do you wish to change? How can you use your imagination to facilitate this change?

2. Imagine yourself preparing to give a sermon. How can you empower those in the audience to use their imagination in ways that encourage them to positively act on your message?

3. Take a moment to pray for someone you frequently pray for. This time try imagining yourself as the person for whom you are praying. How does this change your prayers?

4. What is one of your favorite Bible stories? Take time to imagine yourself as one of the characters in the story and let the story play out in your imagination. Describe your experience.

Chapter 5

The 6-Step Brain Change Program:
Renew Your Mind and
Transform Your Life

We've learned an astounding amount of information about the brain thus far. While I have offered many suggestions and approaches throughout the book on changing our thoughts, emotions, and behaviors, in this final chapter I offer a comprehensive, detailed program for making those changes last. But before we jump into each step of the brain change program itself, let's briefly revisit three fundamental principles from preceding chapters that must be understood in order to make the most of the program: use it or lose it; neurons that fire together, wire together; and imagination becomes reality.

First, when it comes to our brain, we have to "use it or lose it." That is, we have to use the neurons and pathways we want to keep or else we lose them to the brain's natural pruning of dormant, unused neurons (remember our houseplant analogy from Chapter 2?). The neurons and pathways we use frequently grow stronger each time they're activated, which is why the thoughts that come to our mind the fastest are products of our past experiences, practice, and imagination. The effect of these thoughts is that they translate into automatic behaviors, which kick in like computer software whenever we experience a triggering event or circumstance.

Triggers are people places, and things that elicit strong reactions from us, both positive and negative. Some triggers lead to harmful thoughts and behaviors, and if we want to overcome triggers, then we must examine where our thoughts go in times of stress. Does our brain permit negative self-talk, like, *I hate my life. I can't do this,* and does our internal software react to that negativity by leading us to binge on ice cream and hide under our covers? Or does our brain think, *I can handle this. God will provide*, and do we react positively and constructively by throwing away the carton of ice cream and going for a walk instead? Will you write your own software, or will you allow other people and outside forces to write it for you?

Another critical concept to understand about the brain is that "neurons that fire together wire together." We forge links between brain pathways, linking together people, objects, actions, and emotions. An example of this from Chapter 3 is a stoplight. In learning traffic rules, our neurons formed connections between colors and actions: green means go, red means stop, and yellow means slow down. One link that I personally continue to have to prevent from forming relates to my compassion for the very people I work with: the homeless. I've had to shovel human excrement from sidewalks so many times that I have to work hard *not* to associate feelings of disgust with the homeless people responsible for it. I have to consciously choose compassion.

Building off the use-it-or-lose-it and fire-together-wire-together concepts is the power of the imagination in shaping reality. As we learned in Chapter 4, performing an action, perceiving an action, and imagining an action all rely on the same brain paths. So if we imagine ourselves doing good, helping others, and resisting temptation, then we're creating and strengthening pathways in our brain that encourage us to do good, help others, and resist temptation in the real world. We can develop healthy habits, automatic behaviors, and strong morals in our imagination as easily as we do through our actions, and it is in this way that imagination becomes reality.

Lastly before we dive into the brain change program, I must mention an approach to brain change that is similar to mine. It comes from Dr. Caroline Leaf's bestselling book, *Switch On Your Brain: The Key to Peak Happiness, Thinking, and Health*. In it, Leaf offers what she calls a "Brain Detox Program" and advocates following these steps: gather, reflect, write, revisit, reach.[53] Basically, use these steps to first identify the thought we seek to change, reflect on it, replace it with a new one, and then repeat. Despite Dr. Leaf's encouragement to replace destructive thoughts with productive ones, it fell short of my needs.

I felt like I was in a comedy sketch that aired on *MadTV* and guest starred Bob Newhart. In the sketch, a client with a variety of personal issues seeks help from a counselor played by Newhart. Whenever the client mentions something she wants to change about herself, the counselor would yell, "Stop it!" as the solution.

I needed more than just "Stop it!" The question is *how* do I stop it? The same goes for the Scripture. Second Corinthians 10:5 says, "Take every thought captive" (ESV). But how? I needed specific details on how to replace specific thoughts—not only to help myself but also to help those around me.

To better understand how to utilize our brain to effect change, I turned to recent scientific discoveries. To apply that knowledge in such a way to inform our spiritual lives, I turned to the Bible. Together, they gave rise to my six-step brain change program.

Step 1: Identify the Thought

The first step in the brain change program is to identify the thought or behavior you seek to change. If it is a behavior, ask yourself what thought lies behind it and why it motivates you to act. Contemplate this thought or behavior. Break it down. Write about it and identify the elements within your control that you can change. What concepts, experiences, or people does your brain link with this thought or behavior? Brainstorm about them (pun intended).

As an example, let's say you want to change your relationship with alcohol by drinking less often. To identify the thought driving this behavior, think of alcohol as a weed. Then ask yourself which thoughts are feeding that weed and helping it grow. What circumstances compel you to drink more than you'd like? A stressful day at work? Thanksgiving with the in-laws? Or perhaps those thoughts are connected to family problems, unresolved grief, anger, money, guilt, shame, lack of confidence, or something else.

When identifying a problematic thought or behavior, you can be certain that you will have to confront even more complex thoughts, emotions, and behaviors. It is easy to feel overwhelmed by this endeavor, like you've just opened a huge can of worms. But identifying all the different pieces gives you a place to start and lays the foundation for step 2.

> When identifying a problematic thought or behavior, you can be certain that you will have to confront even more complex thoughts, emotions, and behaviors.

Step 2: Evaluate

In the second step, evaluate the thought or behavior. Is it true? Is it necessary? Is the thought normal? Is the thought helpful when considering the big picture? Does it point to something deeper? Does it necessitate an external change in behavior on your part?

Let's apply these evaluative questions to the example in step 1 about changing your relationship with alcohol. Is it true that you drink more than you like? Why do you turn to alcohol when you're with in-laws? Do you feel uncomfortable around them because of an unresolved conflict among all of you? Do you fear social rejection and drink to excess to calm the nerves?

In another example, let's say you feel lonely. Your thought, then, is *I feel lonely*. To evaluate that thought, ask yourself why you feel lonely. Do you lack friends? In asking yourself that question, you might realize that you do have friends and simply need to schedule more time with them than with Netflix. Or maybe you do want more friends. Ask yourself what might be standing in the way of your making friends. Do you project negativity that pushes people away? Evaluate where the negativity comes from. Do you talk *at* people instead of with them? Keep digging to better understand yourself.

Negative thoughts and feelings are completely normal, and not every thought or feeling needs to be challenged or replaced. You can simply listen to your thoughts and feelings instead. If you're afraid of walking past a particular area after dark, for example, rather than attempting to eliminate the fear, listen to it and simply avoid that area at night.

At this stage, our job in evaluating negative thoughts and feelings is not to make them go away, especially since some negative feelings prompt positive action, but to determine whether and what kinds of changes we might need to make.

Step 3: Replace, Don't Resist

Because the willpower approach to change typically fails, don't wrestle with the thought or behavior; that only makes it worse. Dwelling on a bad thought or behavior, even within the context of resisting, strengthens the neurons of that bad thought or behavior. It expands the neural highway. Instead of resisting, do something different!

You must neglect negative thoughts and habits so that the neurons associated with them weaken, and then you must replace those negative thoughts and habits with positive ones so that those neurons can strengthen. Instead of repeating to yourself, *I'm lonely because nobody likes me,* replace that thought with a positive one: *I'm excited to meet new people.* If it's a behavior you seek to change, then replace it with an activity you find enjoyable. Instead of isolating yourself and eating dinner in front of the television, invite a friend to dine with you at one of your favorite restaurants.

You may have to replace a negative thought or behavior again and again but keep at it. Any amount of neglecting the old thing weakens it. We want to focus our thoughts on positivity and living victoriously.

Step 4: Retrain with Imagination

We know the brain can't tell the difference between imagining an action and doing it for real, so take time to imagine and rehearse the good, positive behaviors you wish to establish.

Let's go back to the example in step 1 of changing your relationship with alcohol. Close your eyes and pretend you're at Thanksgiving dinner with your in-laws, who make you feel uneasy. Imagine yourself walking past the bottles of wine and toward the refrigerator. Now imagine yourself opening the refrigerator door and reaching for a carton of eggnog instead. Include as many vivid details as possible in this imaginary situation. How heavy is the carton of eggnog? What smells fill the air? Who's laughing way too loudly?

The more you practice good actions in your mind, the more likely you are to convert those good actions into automatic behaviors.

> The more you practice good actions in your mind, the more likely you are to convert those good actions into automatic behaviors.

Step 5: Introduce a New Element

By this stage, you've identified a thought or behavior you wish to change, and you're working to replace that thought or behavior with a positive one. You're also imagining yourself putting that positive thought or behavior into action, repeating it in your mind until you've programmed it as an automatic behavior. The next step is to disrupt harmful, problematic neural links by introducing new, positive elements and emotions.

Disrupt harmful, problematic neural links by introducing new, positive elements and emotions.

Introducing new elements was a practice I used with clients at the rehab center. At first, they'd tell me how awful and painful it felt to do good things, such as walk away, turn the other cheek, or tell the truth. They were not accustomed to these behaviors and needed to unlink negative feelings from these good actions and relink positive feelings to them instead. To help them create positive associations with good actions, I introduced the element of praise. I made sure to celebrate their actions and encouraged their peers to do the same.

Let's say you feel angry whenever you think of the time you got into a heated argument with your in-laws about where you and your family would spend Thanksgiving. Share the memory of this argument multiple times with people you feel safe with and in places you feel safe. Your brain, over time, will relink feelings of safety to the memory. You could also pray for your in-laws and your relationship with them to introduce positive, constructive feelings. The first time telling a painful story is always uncomfortable, but it will get easier.

Step 6: Repeat, Rehearse, Repeat

You might have heard that you can create a new habit in twenty-one days. This is a myth. You also might have heard that change in the brain takes thirty days. This, too, is a myth. It can take mere moments for a song to get stuck in your head, and it can take forever to remember that one guy's name, what's-his-face.

The amount of time it takes to implement a change varies from person to person. Every brain is different, so change may come more quickly for one person than the person standing next to them. The amount of time it takes to change also depends on how entrenched a belief, thought, or behavior is inside a person's brain.

Neurons take a while to unlink, grow, and form new connections. Remember that you are deconstructing a highway and building a new one. If you start to feel discouraged by how long it's taking you to make a change, revisit earlier steps in the program to see how far you've come. And even if the problematic highway still exists, rejoice over how many concrete slabs you've removed so far.

Repeat each step in the brain change program as many times as you need and for as long as you need, and then keep it up. A professional golfer who's mastered their swing will continue to practice in order to maintain peak performance, and you should do the same for your brain.

The Brain Change Program in Action

When sharing the brain change program with others, I sometimes ask listeners to anonymously write down on a piece of paper a problematic thought or behavior they wish to change. I collect the papers, and then I walk each thought or behavior through all six steps of the program, teaching listeners how to apply the program to their own lives. In this section, I include some of the most common problems I receive.

It should be noted that the proposed solutions to the problems below are not exhaustive and cannot accommodate every person's unique life circumstances. The solutions simply represent one approach, one option, for dealing with problems.

As this book is Christian in nature, I primarily offer solutions that include Scripture verses, using them to help replace a problematic thought or behavior. However, you are not limited to Bible verses. You can explore these problems and develop solutions independently and with the help of a counselor.

I fear public speaking.

I remember the first time I was asked to speak in front of a large group. The content was fine, but I delivered it in a shaky voice and tapped my foot to its own nervous rhythm. Then, when I started working at the rehab center, I learned I would be preaching three times a month. *You mean I have to keep a room of seventy or so addicts, some with ADHD, engaged for an entire sermon?* I thought. *Oh boy.*

I was just as shaky and nervous giving my first sermon as I was during the speaking engagement I mentioned earlier. But because I started to speak regularly, the neurons in my brain got used to it, and I found my own style. With experience, the nervousness faded away until it was gone.

But soon a new problem emerged. I felt like I was doing a lousy job, even if feedback from the audience was overwhelmingly positive. I would replay my sermon in my head over and over, analyzing what I could have done better, what I could have said differently, or what listeners might have misinterpreted. I also realized I had a tendency to single out the most hostile or expressionless audience member, and if I didn't win them over by the end, I felt like I failed.

Obviously, my habit of dwelling on the negative was unhelpful, so I walked it through the brain change program.

1. Identify the Thought: I second guess and criticize myself after speaking to large groups.

2. Evaluate: It is true that it can be helpful to figure out how I can improve, so this aspect of the thought does not need replacement. However, I am needlessly critical of myself, and I want to change this.

3. Replace: Whenever I start to criticize myself after replaying a sermon or conversation in my head, I picture myself opening my hands and watching the self-criticism float away. How people receive and respond to my

sermon is ultimately in God's hands, so I trust him with the results and let it go.

4. Retrain with Imagination: I replace the negative thoughts with mental imagery of the criticism leaving my hands.

5. Introduce a New Element: I thank God for guiding my sermon or conversation and for controlling what happens next. In doing so, I introduce feelings of gratitude and trust.

6. Repeat: I have performed this exercise so many times that letting go of personal criticism is now second nature. As soon as I start to obsess over what I said, the image of hands letting go crops up in my brain.

I'm impatient with my kids.

This, too, is a popular (and personal) problem. Sometimes I get impatient and snappy with my kids when they fuss excessively or if undesirable behaviors persist despite my parenting interventions. When my oldest child told me, "When you get short with me, I don't feel loved or appreciated," I knew I needed to run my problem through the program.

1. Identify the Thought: In thinking through my frustration, I find it stems from feelings of powerlessness. When I can't solve a problem, I respond with irritation.

2. Evaluate: I want to change how I respond to whining and misbehavior because my kids need to feel loved even

when I am correcting them. First Corinthians 13:5 tells me that love is not irritable. Oops, guilt time.

3. Replace: I don't grit my teeth and tell myself not to feel frustrated or angry. Instead, whenever I begin to feel powerless, I tell myself, "I can do all things through Him who strengthens me" (Philippians 4:13 NASB). I remind myself that I am not God, and I do not have to solve everything. I could also replace anger and snippiness with silence, returning to my kids once I've calmed down. Or for times that warrant discipline, I could find an appropriate consequence and deliver it in a loving tone.

4. Retrain with Imagination: I imagine scenarios of my kids fussing and myself responding with care and comfort—crouching down to their level, using a gentle tone, and offering them a hug. I imagine shutting my mouth when my anger starts to bubble up. This links together the concept of frustration with the image of a closed mouth representing patience.

5. Introduce a New Element: I ask my wife to praise and encourage me when I successfully navigate challenging parenting moments with grace and patience.

6. Repeat.

I get upset when I feel disrespected.

I frequently heard this problem from clients, but lots of people have this same problem.

1. Identify the Thought: You experience a strong, negative feeling and/or reaction when others treat you disrespectfully. It's not always the case, but you might have a weak self-concept in the sense that your identity is rooted in what other people think of you. That identity is then threatened when people treat you disrespectfully.

2. Evaluate: You let other people control your emotions and define your identity. This is unhealthy, so it should be addressed by finding a new source for your identity.

3. Replace: Learn and repeat Scripture verses that center on your identity in Christ, such as Psalm 100:3; 139:14, and 1 John 3:1. Reclaim your identity and self-concept from others and find them in positive affirmations found in Jesus.

4. Retrain with Imagination: Think about scenarios in which you react to disrespect with kindness and grace. Imagine God telling you how much he likes you. Sure, it's easy to believe God loves you since it's part of his nature, but imagine him liking you and enjoying your company. Imagine him speaking the Scripture verses you learned in step 3.

5. Introduce a New Element: In imagining God sharing with you the Bible verses about your identity in Christ, you introduce positive emotions to your new self-concept. Surround yourself with people who affirm your new identity in Christ.

6. Repeat.

I get angry about politics.

I once had a friend challenge a group of us to a contest. He told us, "Tell me three words that can ruin Thanksgiving." People said, "Dinner is burned," or "The turkey is tofu." I piped in with, "Let's discuss politics!" I won.

1. Identify the Thought: Where does your political anger come from? Is it from feeling threatened? Unsafe? Helpless? Victimized? Could it be a lack of trust in God's care for the world, regardless of political outcomes?

2. Evaluate: Passion for your political beliefs is not necessarily a bad thing. It shows that your beliefs are important to you and motivate you to act. But when anger rears its ugly head, it makes it difficult to get along with others who believe differently than you. It can also become difficult to treat them with love and respect. You need to address the anger.

3. Replace: Repeat Scripture verses that speak of God's faithfulness regardless of circumstances. No political figure, party, or policy can remove you from God's faithfulness (see Romans 8:39).

4. Retrain with Imagination: Imagine acting lovingly toward people you disagree with politically. Plan ahead by creating automatic loving behaviors that will fire when confronted with disagreements.

5. Introduce a New Element: Pray for people and leaders you disagree with. Introduce positive emotions toward those you might have otherwise considered political adversaries.

6. Repeat.

I get angry with rude, pushy people.

The person who shared this problem gave the example of someone cutting them off in traffic.

1. Identify the Thought: Perhaps your anger comes from assuming the worst about someone's intentions, feeling unsafe or uncomfortable, or violating your boundaries.

2. Evaluate: Anger is a natural reaction to someone putting you at risk or endangering you. You feel compelled to stand up for yourself, but doing so could negatively impact your day or lead to unsafe driving. You can stand up for yourself without turning to anger, and you're more likely to respond in a healthy way if you remove anger from the equation. Anger also gets in the way of practicing empathy. You will want to address your anger and underlying issues.

3. Replace: This is a good opportunity to play the "Reasons Why" game I mentioned in Chapter 3. If you see someone in a hurry, brainstorm ideas (without assigning blame) about why they cut you off. Maybe they're rushing to the hospital because a loved one is having

a medical emergency. Maybe they desperately need a restroom. Over time, you'll find yourself able to empathize instead of assume the worst.

I once had a client who was always rude to me. He disparaged me and called my abilities into question at every turn. I tried to understand why he was treating me so poorly, and we eventually figured it out. I looked somewhat like his father, and his negative emotions linked to his father transferred to me. It seemed odd since this client was significantly older than me, but if he's ten years old in the movie playing in his head and his father was around my age (at the time), it makes sense. By thinking through reasons why this client was rude, I was able to feel empathy and remain calm despite his rudeness.

4. Retrain with Imagination: Imagine yourself getting cut off in traffic again. Instead of cursing or tailgating the driver, imagine yourself taking a deep breath and playing the "Reasons Why" game.

5. Introduce a New Element: Pray for those who are rude and pushy, particularly if you interact with them on a regular basis. You'll introduce positive emotions into the mix, and your actions toward them might encourage the rude person to change their behavior in return.

6. Repeat.

I feel anxious in social situations.

1. Identify the Thought: Where does this insecurity come from? Do you feel socially awkward? Do you fear that if people got to know you, they wouldn't like you? Do you feel unlikable?

2. Evaluate: This insecurity isn't serving you well and should be run through the brain change program.

3. Replace: Memorize and repeat verses about your identity in Christ. When you feel secure in yourself, it's easier to feel secure around others because you're not rooting your identity in their perception of you. And if you embarrass yourself, you can laugh it off because it isn't threatening your core identity.

4. Retrain with Imagination: Imagine yourself enjoying and thriving in social situations. Practice conversing with people you're comfortable around and then progressively engage in more challenging social environments. If you tend to second-guess yourself after social interactions, try the imagination exercise I shared earlier in which you picture yourself holding the conversation in your hands and then letting it go for God to take.

5. Introduce a New Element: First, it may be helpful to realize that lots of people feel anxious and insecure in social situations. You're far from alone in this fear. In fact, when I ask audience members to share the problems they

want to work on, about a quarter of the responses are this very issue. Tell yourself that the person you're talking to might feel just as insecure as you do. Remind yourself that social skills take practice too.

6. Repeat.

I feel insecure about my appearance.

1. Identify the Thought: The core thought is you do not like the way you look and feel embarrassed.

2. Evaluate: You can grow out a bad haircut. A dentist can fix missing or broken teeth. You can exercise and eat better if you're insecure about your body. And while you can alter your appearances in many ways, your confidence and self-worth should not depend on your appearance, so this thought goes into the change program.

3. Replace: Some Bible verses discuss beauty coming from within. Memorize and repeat verses like 1 Samuel 16:7, which talks about how God does not look at outward appearance but rather the heart, or Psalm 139:14, which tells you that you are fearfully and wonderfully made. Repeat these verses in your head, or maybe write them on post-it notes and stick them to your mirror.

4. Retrain with Imagination: Imagine beauty radiating out from your heart.

5. Introduce a New Element: Focus on parts of yourself that you like.

6. Repeat.

I struggle to feel God's closeness and love.

Note that the person who shared this problem was not emotionally close with his father.

1. Identify the Thought: You may lack or distrust God's love for you but also desire to feel it like a father who loves his child.

2. Evaluate: Is it helpful to feel disconnected from God? Nope. It does not spiritually benefit you to feel distant from him. Are there things you can do to draw closer to him? Perhaps you haven't spent enough time with him. This might be hard at first, especially if you don't trust God's love for you, but taking small steps in spending more time in prayer can guide you in a positive direction.

3. Replace: A good verse to introduce to your brain is Romans 8:38–39, which states that nothing can separate us from the love of God. Replace feelings of distance from God with ongoing meditation and repetition of this verse.

4. Retrain with Imagination: Imagine sitting with God and him telling you how much he likes and loves you. Imagine God taking you by the hand and leading you to safety like a shepherd.

5. Introduce a New Element: If this issue stems from your relationship with your own father, pray for him. If he is deceased, pray for insight and understanding as to why he was the way that he was. Some fathers do horrible things, so praying for him can present a significant challenge. Instead of relating to God as a father, you can detour entirely and relate to him in a different way, like seeing him as the Good Shepherd from Psalm 23.

    Another way to introduce trust is to keep a prayer journal. Write down your requests on one side of the page, and then leave room on the other side to write when and how God answered them. Those who have done this exercise are usually surprised to discover just how many requests God answers.

    Again, these steps are not meant to excuse bad behavior but to correct harmful emotional links in your brain so that any one person's bad behavior does not negatively impact your life.

6. Repeat.

I struggle to stand up to others.

1. Identify the Thought: The issue is a lack of boundaries. Could this stem from a lack of confidence or courage? Lacking confidence and courage ultimately goes back to an unstable identity. People who avoid conflict are often more concerned with being liked, so if your core identity

is independent from others, you are more likely to set appropriate boundaries without fearing their reactions.

2. Evaluate: If you struggle to stand up to others because you simply don't know how, learn the steps of addressing interpersonal conflict in Matthew 18 instead of running the issue through the brain change program. If those steps do not lead to improvement or resolution, know that you have God's blessing to no longer interact with them. If your struggle is rooted in a lack of confidence, however, you will want to apply it to the brain change program.

3. Replace: To address issues of confidence, I point people again to Scripture verses regarding their identity in Christ. I also recommend supplementing these with verses on courage and faith in the face of fear. First John 4:18 tells us that perfect love casts out fear, so if you make this kind of love a part of who you are, it becomes an act of love to protect yourself or others during a confrontation.

4. Retrain with Imagination: You might think you should imagine scenarios in which you effectively stand up for yourself or others and manage the conflict in a firm, Christlike way. Do be careful with this approach, as it can easily turn into a preoccupation in which you constantly reword what you plan to say long into the night. In that case, you're not training your brain; you're worrying

obsessively. Tough conversations rarely go as planned, so memorizing everything you want to say in future conversations probably won't work.

The automatic program approach, however, can work in helping you start the conversation. Imagine yourself speaking up during a conflict and a resulting positive outcome. If you approach a conflict thinking, *This will end in disaster*, then you risk a self-fulfilling prophecy. Tell yourself that the conversation will improve your relationship.

5. Introduce a New Element: Pray forward for those with whom you have conflict and for future conversations necessitating godly confrontation. In developing positive feelings toward conflict resolution, you're better able to engage these uncomfortable conversations in a loving way.

6. Repeat.

I am irresponsible with money.

1. Identify the Thought: What do you spend your money on and when? What do you get out of it? Is it retail therapy? Does it stem from wanting to keep up with other people's lifestyles? Is it impulse spending?

2. Evaluate: This thought indicates that a change in lifestyle is needed, but the issue is how to get there in thought and action. A wish to be more responsible is a good thought

that prompts you to change whatever thinking lies beneath the irresponsibility.

3. Replace: Repeat to yourself, *I am a steward. God has given me this money to manage. The money is not mine.*

4. Retrain with Imagination: Imagine giving a daily report to God on how you managed money that day. Imagine scenarios of spending money in a godly way.

    I refer back to the client from Chapter 3 who said he'd spend money on drugs and prostitutes if he were to receive a large sum. To retrain him, we had him imagine saving money and spending it on basic necessities like food, shelter, and his health. Then we gave him small amounts of money as an allowance to help him practice spending wisely.

5. Introduce a New Element: Pray before spending. This will deter reckless spending by forcing you to pause and redirect as needed. You could also make a rule for yourself that you have to wait twenty-four hours before buying something that isn't a basic need.

6. Repeat.

My chronic pain leaves me irritable.

This one caught me off guard. Could the brain change program help people cope with chronic pain? It turns out it can! This does not mean that your pain isn't real or simply in your head. Of course the pain is real and most likely has a physical cause.

But since pain has both physical and psychological components, your attitude can affect the degree of pain you feel.

If your thoughts run along the lines of *This pain prevents me from working, getting around, and sleeping*, then this belief may translate to behaviors that magnify the pain. If you deem yourself helpless, dwell on negative thoughts, or anticipate worst-case scenarios, it results in more intense pain[54] and higher levels of fatigue.[55] For example, if you suffer an injury on the job and hate your job, you are more likely to be disabled by your injury than if you like your job.[56] Additionally, the stress involved with pain produces chemicals in your brain that make your experience of the pain even worse.

1. Identify the Thought: You regularly experience pain, which makes it difficult to be kind, patient, and empathetic. What is your attitude toward your pain? Do you feel helpless, anxious, negative, without purpose, or hopeless? In a journal, keep track of your thoughts and feelings about your pain throughout the day to identify thought patterns you might need to change.

2. Evaluate: You want to be nicer, but you also accept the pain as a given. You could focus on the "be nicer" part, but if you change how you experience the pain, then being nicer will probably become easier. The pain remains, but your change in attitude can help manage your pain and your behavior.[57] You could also work with a therapist or psychologist who specializes in cognitive

behavioral therapy if you find changing your thoughts on your own is too challenging.

3. Replace: Research has shown that if you don't fear pain or dwell on negative thoughts about it, the pain is more manageable and less frequent. A good verse to begin with is Philippians 4:13, which states that with God you can do all things. *With God, I am victorious over my pain* and *I can manage my pain* are phrases to repeat to yourself to help overcome feelings of helplessness and hopelessness. Replace *I can't cope* with *I can cope!*

4. Retrain with Imagination: Pray through Psalm 23, imagining God leading you through a dangerous valley that represents your pain. Imagine yourself enjoying physical activities and then try them. You could also imagine best-case scenarios to override catastrophic thinking, or anticipating the worst to happen.

5. Introduce a New Element: Here I suggest introducing not a new element but an old element. Think about how you used to move before the injury. Do this enough and you can reactivate brain pathways that eroded over time from lack of use (remember use it or lose it). This will give you a greater sense of control over your pain and hopefully reduce stress.

6. Repeat.

I overeat.

1. Identify the Thought: When do you overeat? How does overindulging in food make you feel? Do you overeat in an attempt to fill a void? Do you eat when you feel depressed? Stressed? Once you identify what lies behind the overeating, you can take that thought through the brain change program. Let's say you overeat because of stress.

2. Evaluate: Regular, ongoing stress releases a hormone called cortisol, which increases your appetite. And it's true that some foods, particularly sugary and fatty ones, reduce stress in the short term (we invented the term "comfort food" for a reason).

   The desire to change your eating habits will likely prompt you to make some changes, such as limiting the availability of certain foods in your home or avoiding the bakery or fast-food chains. But if you avoid addressing the reasons for your overeating, your changes are unlikely to stick.

3. Replace: Read Matthew 6:25–34, which tells us that God takes care of sparrows and birds, and since we are of greater value, we can find peace knowing he takes care of us in greater measure.

4. Retrain with Imagination: To combat stress with hope, whether related to eating or otherwise, picture lilies in your mind as a reminder of the verses in Matthew. Imagine

yourself driving past your favorite burger place, choosing a healthier option when dining out, or distracting yourself with an activity when an urge to overindulge strikes.

5. Introduce a New Element: Practice thankfulness to remind yourself of God's faithfulness. Our family takes time every night before bed to tell each other things for which we were thankful that day. Keeping a journal of things you're grateful for is another option.

6. Repeat.

I can't forgive myself.

1. Identify the Thought: You are experiencing unresolved guilt.

2. Evaluate: If you have not sought forgiveness, then thoughts of guilt are a signal that you need to make an important change. Repent and seek forgiveness for the wrongs you have done, then carry any remaining feelings of guilt into the brain change program.

3. Replace: There's plenty of secular advice on how to forgive yourself, but guess what? The Bible says nothing about forgiving yourself—because you can't. Stop trying! In attempting to forgive yourself or minimize your wrongs, you're attempting to assume the role of God. It is not up to you to determine what is and isn't a sin or

its severity. The solution to unresolved guilt is accepting forgiveness granted to you by God through Jesus.

Replace the condemnation of yourself with God's acceptance. Memorize verses about forgiveness and repeat them when negative feelings arise. For a starting place, read Psalm 103:10, Psalm 32:1–7, and Matthew 6:9–15.

To momentarily digress from the steps, it's possible that unresolved guilt may not actually be guilt at all but regret. In this case, you walk in forgiveness, but you also grieve lost opportunities, consequences, and what could have been. My clients with long-term addictions and criminal records have to face the reality that they probably won't land the same job as a peer who worked for the last decade. Family and friends may not want to reconcile, and if they do, it may not be on the timetable my clients wish for.

Perhaps unresolved guilt over what you have done has morphed into shame. This denotes a shift in thinking from *I have done something bad* to *I am bad*. Again, accept God's forgiveness and focus on your true identity in Christ.

For situations of regret, I refer to Joel 2:24–26, in which God tells a formerly disobedient Israel that he will restore what the locusts have eaten. Their sin brought famine and calamity, but God promised that once they got their act together, he would create something new. They would have new crops. Memorize these verses to shift your focus from what you lost or missed out on what you will create with God going forward. It probably won't be a return to what you had, but it will be new and good.

4. Retrain with Imagination: In the case of feeling unforgiven, imagine God embracing you and telling you that he accepts you. Picture yourself as the prodigal son, returning home to a joyful father. In the case of regret, return to the image of holding it in your hands and letting it float away to God. Picture yourself building a future and start with what you have now. Going off the locust verse in Joel 2:24–26, imagine a barren field becoming green again.

5. Introduce a New Element: The imagination exercises in step four will introduce hope, link positive emotions with forgiveness, and overwrite guilt and regret.

6. Repeat.

I don't use my time effectively.

People often report that they wish they spent less time watching television, scrolling on their phones, playing video games, and other unproductive activities. They want to spend more time reading the Bible, praying, and getting work done.

1. Identify the Thought: Many people characterize this problem as laziness, but laziness comes from somewhere. Are you depressed and using entertainment to cope? Do your tasks feel so overwhelming that it seems easier to avoid them? What mental, emotional, and situational

barriers might be interfering with your ability to accomplish desired tasks? Fear of failure? Confused about where to start? I recommend that you stop using the "lazy" label. You are "lazy" for a reason. Find that reason and address it.

2. Evaluate: You have a desire to make an external change in how you spend your time. This change would positively impact your life, so it's well suited for the brain change program.

3. Replace: A myriad of reasons may contribute to "laziness," and while I can't address all of them, I can offer a few pointers to help you address them appropriately.

   If you are trying to take on too much, your brain will easily fall back into the time wasting it is familiar with, so start small and build up. One idea is to set an alarm for ten minutes and work on your task during that time. Then give yourself a short break. Then set another alarm. These small steps and practice will strengthen your ability to be productive for longer stretches of time.

   You can also break down complex tasks into smaller ones. I know a professor who broke down his golf swing into forty-eight distinct steps. I am not a golfer, and I have no idea how a person can come up with forty-eight steps for swinging a stick, but it worked for him. Author Anne Lamott, in her book *Bird by Bird*, uses the title of her book as a motivational phrase. How do you count an entire flock of birds? It seems overwhelming, so count them bird by bird instead. One at a time.[58]

4. Retrain with Imagination: One technique that helps me use my time wisely is to start my day imagining myself doing my work successfully. This primes a mindset of completion and motivates me to make it a reality.

5. Introduce a New Element: Reward yourself when you complete a task. Or better yet, reward yourself for completing the steps in the task, to dovetail with the "bird by bird" idea, instead of focusing on completing the entire task. Pat yourself on the back frequently. Think positively: *I can get this done. I will find a way to do it.* Make boring or unpleasant tasks, like cleaning, more manageable with music or an audiobook.

6. Repeat.

I fear the future.

1. Identify the Thought: You fear what the future might bring and its uncertainty.

2. Evaluate: When it is not debilitating, a fear of the future can prompt positive action toward greater success, whether that's earning more money, better supporting a family, or improving your health. However, a life should be lived in faith, not fear.

3. Replace: Just as I mentioned in the issue of overeating, I recommend Matthew 6:25–34. These verses offer reassurance that God takes care of the sparrows and birds, and because we are of greater value, we can find peace knowing he takes care of us in greater measure.

4. Retrain with Imagination: Imagine a future in which you are successful. Create a vivid mental picture of a lily or sparrow and visualize it during times of stress to remind you that God cares for you and looks after you.

5. Introduce a New Element: Pray for what you are running toward, not what you are running from. Pray for the good things that your future may hold. Keep a prayer journal and record times when God has come through for you in powerful ways.

   I once experienced a season of ongoing depression. I dreaded going to work even though it was personally meaningful to me. I prayed and asked God to help me, and one morning, while waiting in my car at an intersection, I felt the depression disappear. And it never came back. I still feel sad and even depressed sometimes, but God removed that particular season of depression. The intersection itself has become my memorial of this event. Whenever I wait at that stoplight, I look at the street names and remember God's faithfulness.

6. Repeat.

I want to stop negative thoughts.

1. Identify the Thought: Two issues surface with this problem. The first issue is the negative thoughts. What sort of negative thoughts are they? Are they criticism of others or criticism of yourself? The second problem is the verbalization of negative thoughts.

    I often verbalize what I think are humorous thoughts before considering how my audience will receive them. For example, my kid's kindergarten teacher assigned each student to bring one hundred items to participate in counting games. I told one parent, "This is great. I cleaned out all the old meds in our bathroom cabinet." The parents within earshot panicked, and I had to stop them from running into the school. We all need to check ourselves sometimes.

2. Evaluate: Negative thoughts do not serve you well or improve your life, and in verbalizing them, you risk ostracizing and potentially offending the people around you. This issue is a good candidate for the brain change program.

3. Replace: Brainstorm positive statements and compliments to keep in your pocket instead of harsh, critical, or negative words. Regarding the verbalization of negative thoughts, a helpful verse is from James 1:19, which tells us to be quick to listen and slow to speak.

4. Retrain with Imagination: Think of someone you see on a fairly regular basis who's not exactly your favorite person. Imagine yourself telling them something nice.

5. Introduce a New Element: A new element might be to give yourself a few seconds before responding to someone in order to break the neural chain between thought and speech.

6. Repeat.

My thoughts wander during prayer.

1. Identify the Thought: Here the problem is not a single thought but lots of thoughts interfering during times of prayer. Maybe your mind replays conversations you had throughout the day, dwells on past experiences, reviews tomorrow's agenda, or contemplates how to survive a tornado of sharks. It could be anything!

2. Evaluate: If you attempt to get serious about prayer, you will likely experience wandering thoughts. So when you ask yourself, "Is this normal?" the answer is yes. This "thought problem" is common and can be a source of embarrassment and frustration. Ask yourself why you have a hard time concentrating. Look for a deeper cause of your distraction.

3. Replace…or Not?. First, be patient with yourself. As you grow in prayer, your ability to focus will likely grow as

well. Replacing wandering thoughts takes time. You have to wrestle with your mind and redirect your thoughts, again and again, to where you wish them to be.

In his book *Life Together*, Dietrich Bonhoeffer talks about this very issue and offers a special prayer hack to bypass this struggle. He suggests that rather than letting the wandering thoughts usher in anxiety or discouragement, try to snatch them back calmly and "incorporate into prayer the people and the events to which our thoughts keep straying."[59] Pray about whatever it is your mind is wandering to. Maybe that wandering thought is actually God's way of directing you toward the very thing you need to pray for.

Replaying events from the day? Pray through them. Thinking about a friend or relative? Pray for them. Scheduling your plans for tomorrow? Talk about your schedule with God. In doing this, you bring prayer with you on the various brain paths you travel. Then, wherever your mind goes, prayer is there as well.

4. Retrain with Imagination: As I talked about earlier, your imagination can contribute to a vibrant prayer life, such as imagining yourself as the person you are praying for or praying in images when you don't have the words. Praying words engages the language centers of the brain, and if you add imagination, you begin to activate other areas of the brain and leave less room for intrusive thoughts.

5. Introduce a New Element: If your traditional way of praying is challenging, spice up your prayer life with variety. Research different methods of prayer. Pray the prayers of Christians throughout history, pray Scripture, have a prayer walk, pray with a partner, pray out loud, or attempt a prayer of examen where you review your day with God.

6. Repeat.

The Fight Phase

When we first begin to change our thoughts and behaviors, we enter what I call the "honeymoon phase." Enthusiasm is high, everything is new, and change seems to come easily. We're not yet asking our brain for deep, lasting neuronal change. The brain thinks, *This is a novel diversion only necessitating minor adjustments. Fun!* Little does our brain know, however, that we have different plans; we are committed to change. Once our brain realizes this and reality sets in, we enter the "fight phase."

When we're in the fight phase, we must first recognize that this phase exists and requires effort. We will likely struggle with making positive changes, and our old ways of thinking and doing will continue to rear their ugly heads. That's why we want to avoid making too many changes at once; we're more likely to become overwhelmed and lose motivation. Instead, we want to focus on each and every win, and as the number of wins accumulates, winning becomes easier because our brain continues to form and strengthen new pathways, relenting to whatever change we're making. Changing your brain is a fight, and your brain will fight back.

> Changing your brain is a fight, and your brain will fight back.

It can also be helpful to seek help from others. We can establish a support group to cheer us on. Depending on the issue, we may want to consider entering a full-on treatment program. Our treatment facility was several miles out of town, so if someone entered the fight phase in the middle of treatment, they had a long walk ahead of them through farmland if they chose to give up the fight. The distance served as a natural obstacle that often made giving up too hard in the moment.

There are benefits to putting obstacles in the way of personal failure. Clean the sugar out of the cabinets, cut off the internet, whatever we need to do to get serious with the problem at hand. Matthew 5:30 even says to cut our hand off if it causes us to sin. What I take from this is that we must be so committed to change that we're prepared to make hard decisions. When I was learning a foreign language, the threat of a big fat *F* grade motivated me to do the work.

> We must be so committed to change that we're prepared to make hard decisions.

While I prefer positive reinforcement in the forms of receiving encouragement from others and rewarding myself when I succeed, negative reinforcement works too. We can remind ourselves what will happen if we fail: *What are the consequences? How will I feel if I give up? How will I feel if I succeed? What will result from my success?*

I return to the exercise "Where does that road lead" described in Chapter 4, where we imagine an action to its completion and the consequences, positive or negative, that come with it. Sometimes we need to resist the immediate gratification of a destructive decision and consider its long-term consequences. On the flip side, we can imagine all the good that may come from making a positive decision.

When we recognize that we are in the fight phase, it is important we don't feel discouraged if and when we fail. When learning that foreign language, I sometimes chose a distraction instead of attending to my large pile of homework. It was important for me not to let the momentary failure develop into a sense of total defeat. "Getting back on the horse" may be a cliché, but it is true. Remember that expanding a small deer path into a highway while simultaneously dismantling the fast, destructive highway takes time, effort, and a continual return to the construction at hand.

Once we feel like we're getting into a groove and changes are becoming second nature, we begin the final phase of making a life change: maintenance. Several dangers come with this phase. The first danger is discouragement. Failures in this stage can sting more than those in the fight phase. We might think, *I was doing so well until this. I'm clearly incapable of change, so I should just throw in the towel.* If this happens, we have to throw ourselves back into the fight phase, not the I-give-up phase. If we stew in feelings of failure, our brain will build back up old, destructive pathways. The faster we move on from feelings of failure, the better we preserve the constructive paths we've worked so hard to build.

The faster we move on from feelings of failure, the better we preserve the constructive paths we've worked so hard to build.

An item to note is that elements contributing to our success may be linked to a routine of ours. But if our routine is disrupted, it may become more difficult to maintain our new, healthier way of living. Examples of disruptions could be a vacation, a job change, or a loss. Anticipate disruptions and get ahead of them by training for success in the imagination. Think of setbacks as a return to the fight phase, which we already overcame once and will overcome again.

Two other similar elements to watch for in the maintenance stage are complacency and overconfidence. We convince ourselves we have it all together and that the positive change is permanent. We focus so much on our success that we deem failure impossible. A real-life case of this comes from a former client who was an alcoholic looking for housing. "Sure, my new roommate has a full bar set up in the living room, but I am cured now," he believed. "This won't bother me. Plus the rent is good."

"Who cares about the rent when your sobriety is more important?" I asked him. "Rent somewhere else."

He didn't listen to my advice. After a few months of successfully avoiding alcohol, he relapsed, moved out, and had to work hard to return to sober living.

If we're on a winning streak, we have no reason to test ourselves on how close we can circle the chasm of failure without falling in. Stay as far away from the chasm as possible.

Escaping the Flames

One day at the rehabilitation farm, everyone woke to a great shout: "Fire! Fire!"

One of our residents had accidentally flicked a cigarette into a hay pile. A fire started and spread rapidly. As the flames reached the pig barn housing sows and their piglets, the residents arrived at the scene. The animals' panicked squeals compelled several residents to run into the burning barn and rescue the pigs and their little piglets.

The residents, on-site staff, and the pigs gathered out front, watching the barn now fully engulfed. Then, all of a sudden, a group of pigs sped off, running back into the barn before we could stop them. The fire had spread too far by then, and we could not save them. They had run to their deaths.

The residents were devastated. They had cared for those pigs from birth, and some of the residents had even delivered them as piglets. The residents risked their lives to save them. Why would the pigs run back into a burning barn?

In times of stress, pigs (and people) run to what is familiar, even if it is destructive—even if it kills them. The barn was familiar to the pigs, and in their fear, the barn represented safety even though it was in flames.

How many times have you been rescued only to run back into a burning barn? How often do you continue to do things that harm and destroy you, leaving those around you to suffer the pain of your decisions? Brains crave what they already know. For the pigs, that meant their barn. What does your brain crave?

Brains crave what they already know.

Summary

We must reshape our brain to run toward good things, constructive things, things that benefit self and others, not the flames of self-destruction. We also need to understand the brains of those whom we try to rescue and not feel discouraged when we see them run back into their burning barn.

May we all work with God to create the brains, thoughts, and actions that keep us and others running away from burning barns and toward that which is good, right, loving, and life giving.

As I mentioned in the preface and introduction, discoveries in neuroscience, many of which we've discussed in this book, helped me answer my questions and led me to my own discovery: we can change our brain and free ourselves from destructive thoughts and harmful behaviors and toward that which produces the fruit of the Spirit: love, joy, peace, patience, kindness, goodness, faithfulness, gentleness, and self-control. With God, we truly have the power to renew our minds and transform our lives.

> With God, we truly have the power to renew our minds and transform our lives.

Reflect

1. Think back to the brain map you created in Chapter 2. Create a new brain map representing how you want your brain to function. This map can guide you wherever you want to travel with your brain change program and, ultimately, your destination.

2. Write down a thought problem you wish to change. Develop your plan for change using the six steps of the brain change program discussed in this chapter: identify, evaluate, replace, retrain with imagination, introduce a new element, and repeat.

3. How have you or someone you know run back into a burning barn in the face of uncertainty? How does thinking about brain change and its desire for familiarity help you?

Acknowledgments

I am grateful to my agent, Julie Gwinn, for believing in this project and Nina Rose for her excellent editorial work.

I offer my heartfelt thanks to Javane Taylor-Strong and Kenneth Shaw for consistently and faithfully praying for me and for this project.

And most of all, thank you to my wife and children, whose love, humor, and sacrifice helped me along the way. Without you, this book would not have been possible.

Endnotes

1   Alicia Juarrero, *Dynamics in Action: Intentional Behavior as a Complex System* (Cambridge, MS: MIT Press, 1999), 53.

2   Eleanor A. Maguire et al., "Navigation-related Structural Change in the Hippocampi of Taxi Drivers," *Proceedings of the National Academy of Sciences* 97, no. 8 (March 2000): 4398–4403.

3   Marc Bangert and Gottfried Schlaug, "Specialization of the Specialized in Features of External Human Brain Morphology," *European Journal of Neuroscience* 24, no. 6 (September 2006): 1832–4.

4   See Vanessa Sluming et al., "Voxel-Based Morphometry Reveals Increased Gray Matter Density in Broca's Area in Male Symphony Orchestra Musicians," *Neuroimage* 17, no. 3 (November 2002): 1613–22; Vanessa Sluming et al., "Broca's Area Supports Enhanced Visuospatial Cognition in Orchestral Musicians," *The Journal of Neuroscience: The Official Journal of the Society for Neuroscience* 27, no. 14 (April 2007): 3799–806.

5   Jens Haueisen and Thomas R. Knosche, "Involuntary Motor Activity in Pianists Evoked by Music Perception," *Journal of Cognitive Neuroscience* 13, no. 6 (August 2001): 786–92.

6   A. D'Ausilio et al., "Cross-Modal Plasticity of the Motor Cortex While Listening to a Rehearsed Musical Piece,"

European Journal of Neuroscience 24, no. 3 (August 2006): 955–58.

7   Donald Watanabe, Tal Savion-Lemieux, and Virginia. B. Penhune, "The Effect of Early Musical Training on Adult Motor Performance: Evidence for a Sensitive Period in Motor Learning," *Experimental Brain Research* 176, no. 2 (January 2007): 332–40.

8   Bogdan Draganski et al., "Neuroplasticity: Changes in Grey Matter Induced by Training," *Nature* 427, no. 6972 (January 2004): 311–12.

9   Tod Perry, "Woman asks Twitter for 'the best thing you learned at therapy' and the responses are life-changing," Upworthy, November 26, 2019, www.upworthy.com.

10   See James Van Slyke et al., *Theology and the Science of Moral Action: Virtue Ethics, Exemplarity, and Cognitive Neuroscience* (New York: Routledge, 2012) for discussions on exemplars not struggling over ethical decisions and feeling they could not have done otherwise.

11   Gregory Peterson, "Exemplarism: Some Considerations," in *Theology and the Science of Moral Action: Virtue Ethics, Exemplarity, and Cognitive Neuroscience*, ed. James Van Slyke et al. (New York: Routledge, 2012), 88.

12   Donald B. Kraybill, Steven M. Nolt, and David Weaver-Zercher, *Amish Grace: How Forgiveness Transcended Tragedy* (San Francisco, CA: Jossey-Bass, 2007).

13   See Chapters 5–9 in Donald B. Kraybill, Steven M. Nolt, and David Weaver-Zercher, *Amish Grace: How Forgiveness*

Transcended Tragedy (San Francisco, CA: Jossey-Bass, 2007).

14   See Chapter 5 in Norman Doidge, *The Brain that Changes Itself* (New York: Penguin Books, 2007).

15   Joseph LeDoux, *Synaptic Self: How Our Brains Become Who We Are* (New York: Penguin Group, 2003), 146.

16   Carla Shatz, "The Developing Brain," *Scientific American* 267, no. 3 (September 1992); 60–67.

17   Gregory L. Gerdeman et al., "It Could Be Habit Forming: Drugs of Abuse and Striatal Synaptic Plasticity," *Trends in Neuroscience* 26, no. 4 (April 2003): 189.

18   Allan Coppedge, *Portraits of God* (Downer's Grove, IL: Intervarsity Press, 2001).

19   Carroll E. Izard et al., "Self Organization of Discrete Emotions, Emotion Patterns, and Emotion-Cognition Relations," In *Emotion, Development, and Self-Organization: Dynamic Systems Approaches to Emotional Development*, eds. Marc D. Lewis and Isabela Granic (Cambridge: Cambridge University Press, 2000), 21.

20   Abraham Maslow, *The Psychology of Science* (New York: Harper & Row, 1966), 15.

21   Abraham Kaplan, *The Conduct of Inquiry: Methodology for Behavioral Science* (San Francisco: Chandler Publishing Company, 1964), 28.

22   Shelley E. Taylor and Jennifer Crocker, "Schematic Bases of Social Information Processing," in *Social Cognition: The*

Ontario Symposium on Personality and Social Psychology, eds. E. Tory Higgins, C. Peter Herman, and Mark P. Zanna (Hillsdale, NJ: Erlbaum, 1981), 89–134.

23   Amber L. Story, "Self-Esteem and Memory for Favorable and Unfavorable Personality Feedback," *Personality and Social Psychology Bulletin* 24, no. 1 (1998): 51–64.

24   John A. Bargh and Tanya L. Chartrand, "The Unbearable Automaticity of Being," *American Psychologist* 54, no. 7 (1999): 473.

25   Victor Cicirelli, "Emotion and Cognition in Attachment," in *Handbook of Emotion, Adult Development, and Aging*, ed. Carol Magai and Susan H. McFadden (San Diego: Academic Press, 1996, 125.

26   For example, subjects who failed or succeeded on a prior, irrelevant task did worse or better on a test afterward indicating that the created mood enhanced or diminished later success. Tanya Chartrand, Amy Dalton, and Clara Cheng, "The Antecedents and Consequences of Nonconscious Goal Pursuit," in *Handbook of Motivation Science*, eds. James Shah and Wendi Gardner (New York: Guilford Press, 2008), 353.

27   Wickliffe Abraham, "Memory Maintenance: The Changing Nature of Neural Mechanisms," *Current Directions in Psychological Science* 15, no. 1 (February 2006): 5–8.

28   Rachel Herz, *The Scent of Desire: Discovering Our Enigmatic Sense of Smell* (New York: Harper Perennial, 2007).

29   See Marcella Althaus-Reid, "Gustavo Gutierrez Goes to Disneyland: Theme Park Theologies and the Diaspora of the Discourse of the Popular Theologian in Liberation Theology," in *Interpreting Beyond Borders*, ed. Fernando Segovia (Sheffield, UK: Sheffield Academic Press, 2000).

30   Bruno Laeng and Unni Sulutvedt, "The Eye Pupil Adjusts to Imaginary Light," *Psychological Science* 25, no. 1 (November 2013): 188–97.

31   Lokman Wong et al., "On the Relationship between the Execution, Perception, and Imagination of an Action," *Behavioral Brain Research* 257, no. 15 (November 2013): 242–52.

32   Some differences exist, especially when the action in question is of a complexity that exceeds the capacity of imagination. See Catherine L. Reed, "Chronometric Comparisons of Imagery to Action: Visualizing Versus Physically Performing Springboard Dives," *Memory and Cognition* 30, no. 8 (2002): 1169–78.

33   I focus on describing similar neural activations among perception, imagination, and action performance, yet I avoid the term *mirror neurons*, which are neurons discovered in primates that activate both when perceiving an action and doing an action. The neuron "mirrors" the behavior of another. I avoid the term because the concept of mirror neurons is controversial. See Gregory Hickok, "Eight Problems for the Mirror Neuron Theory of Action Understanding in Monkeys and Humans," *Journal of Cognitive Neuroscience* 21, no. 7 (July 2009): 1229–43. The

term *mirror neurons* conjures the image of specialized neurons devoted to mimicry, while I believe that many neural assemblies and pathways used in performing an action could be activated in perception and imagination, rather than a specific, specialized system.

34   Vittorio Gallese, "Mirror Neurons and Intentional Attunement: Commentary on Olds," *Journal of the American Psychoanalytic Association* 54, no. 1 (2006): 47–57.

35   See Matthew 5:22, 28.

36   A. Pascual-Leone et al., "Modulation of Muscle Responses Evoked by Transcranial Magnetic Stimulation during the Acquisition of New Fine Motor Skills," *Journal of Neurophysiology* 74, no. 3 (September 1995): 1037.

37   G. Yue and K. J. Cole, "Strength Increases from the Motor Program: Comparison of Training with Maximal Voluntary and Imagined Muscle Contractions," Journal of Neurophysiology 67, no. 5 (May 1992): 1114–23.

38   Catherine L. Reed, "Chronometric Comparisons of Imagery to Action: Visualizing versus Physically Performing Springboard Dives," *Memory & Cognition* 30, no. 8 (2002): 1169.

39   Salvatore Aglioti et al., "Action Anticipation and Motor Resonance in Elite Basketball Players," *Nature Neuroscience* 11, no. 9 (October 2008): 1109–16.

40   Aglioti, "Action Anticipation," 1114.

41 B. Calvo-Merino et al., "Action Observation and Acquired Motor Skills: An fMRI Study with Expert Dancers," *Cerebral Cortex* 15, no. 8 (August 2005): 1243–49.

42 Nancy Sherman, "Character Development and Aristotelian Virtue," in *Virtue Ethics and Moral Education*, eds. David Carr and J. W. Steutel (London: Routledge, 1999), 38.

43 Charlene Burns, "Hardwired for Drama? Theological Speculations on Cognitive Science, Empathy, and Moral Exemplarity," in *Theology and the Science of Moral Action: Virtue Ethics, Exemplarity, and Cognitive Neuroscience*, ed. James Van Slyke et al. (New York: Routledge, 2012), 149–163.

44 Jeremy Hsu, "The Secrets of Storytelling," *Scientific American* 19, no. 4 (August 2008): 46–51.

45 Burns, 155.

46 Alasdair MacIntyre, *After Virtue: A Study in Moral Theory* (Notre Dame, ID: University of Notre Dame Press, 2007), 216.

47 Al Hsu, "Spoiler Alert: The Harry Potter Craze Suggests We're Not Telling the Christian Story Right," *Christianity Today* (website), August 2, 2007, www.christianitytoday.com.

48 Al Hsu, "Spoiler Alert."

49 "Gospel Contemplation – A Fuller Explanation," Orientations for Spiritual Growth," orientations.jesuits.ca.

50 "Gospel Contemplation – A Fuller Explanation."

51   "Healing of Memories for Oneself," *Orientations for Spiritual Growth*, orientations.jesuits.ca.

52   For example, Christian Science claims that the mind is the only reality and that the material world is an illusion that you can change with powerful enough thoughts and imagination, with living in perfect health and even immortality as a possibility if only you "think correctly." Mary Baker Eddy, *Science and Health* (Bedford, MA: Applewood Books, 1875), 292–376.

53   Dr. Caroline Leaf, *Switch On Your Brain: The Key to Peak Happiness, Thinking, and Health* (Grand Rapids, MI: Baker Books, 2013).

54   Robert R. Edwards et al., "Pain, Catastrophizing, and Depression in the Rheumatic Diseases," *Nature Reviews Rheumatology* 7, no. 4 (April 2011): 216–24; Ran Kremer et al., "The Role of Pain Catastrophizing in the Prediction of Acute and Chronic Postoperative Pain," *Open Pain Journal* 6 (July 2013): 176–82.

55   Nada Lukkahatai and Leorey Saligan, "Association of Catastrophizing and Fatigue: A Systematic Review," *Journal of Psychosomatic Research* 74, no. 2 (February 2013): 100–109.

56   M. C. Ratinaud et al. "Job Satisfaction Evaluation in Low Back Pain: A Literature Review and Tools Appraisal," *Annals of Physical and Rehabilitation Medicine* 56, no. 6 (September 2013): 465–81.

57   Marina Shpaner et al., "Unlearning Chronic Pain: A Randomized Controlled Trail to Investigate Changes in Intrinsic Brain Connectivity Following Cognitive Behavioral Therapy," *Neuroimage Clinic* 5 (July 2014): 365–76.

58   Anne Lamott, *Bird by Bird* (New York: Pantheon Books, 1994).

59   Dietrich Bonhoeffer, *Life Together* (New York: Harper & Row Publishers, 1954), 85.

About the Author

After receiving an education in biology and at seminary, Dr. Alan Weissenbacher worked for the Denver Rescue Mission as a chaplain to the homeless. He helped move homeless and addicted people out of an urban setting to a one-hundred-acre farm, giving them opportunities to help run the farm, care for animals, and receive therapy tailored to their individual needs: counseling, addiction therapy, job training, and more.

Inspired by the struggles of his clients and filled with the desire to improve Christian rehabilitation, Alan resigned from his position at the Denver Rescue Mission and enrolled in a doctorate program. He studied neuroscience and spiritual formation at the Center for Theology and the Natural Sciences in Berkeley and engaged with the question of how to improve addiction recovery, church practices, and spiritual formation using the scientific knowledge of the brain.

Alan serves as the managing editor for the academic journal *Theology and Science* and has published works with Johns Hopkins University Press, Vernon Press, and ATF Press on the subjects of science, religion, and ethics. He authored the chapter on neuroscience and the human person in the second edition of the college textbook *Science and Religion: A Historical Introduction* in addition to articles in several journals, including *Theology and Science, Dialog, Wesleyan Theological Journal*, and *Zygon*.

Alan currently works as a stay-at-home dad to two young boys while he writes, guest lectures, consults, and bakes cool themed cakes for his kids (the fire-breathing dragon cake is their favorite to date).